To Liz
From Liz!

Downton

the town that
became a village

Elizabeth Hutchinson

To my mother

The Hobnob Press
30c Deverill Road Trading Estate, Sutton Veny, Warminster BA12 7BZ
07715 620790
Spire Books
South Barn, Old Standlynch Farm, Downton, Salisbury SP5 3QR
01722 711665
and

www.hobnobpress.co.uk

CIP data: a catalogue record for this book is available from the
British Library
Designed by John Elliott
ISBN 978-1-906978-33-4
Photographs by Graham Hutchinson unless otherwise acknowledged.

Contents

Harry Hepper, Downton railway station master sells the last ticket to Sue Grice (Julia Whitmarsh).

Foreword

MICHAEL WOOD

Downton. The name is known across the world now through the long running television drama which took viewers from the Edwardian era through the traumas of the First World War and into the uncertain interwar years. That Downton was the story of a grand country house, the old world of aristocratic privilege, of *Upstairs Downstairs*. But far fewer people will know that the real life Downton is a large and historic Wiltshire village on the Hampshire border a few miles south of Salisbury. With its attached hamlets of Witherington, Standlynch, Redlynch and Charlton, it is a place of amazing continuities. It has probably been inhabited continuously from the Stone Age; during the Roman empire it had a villa with a fine mosaic; it was the centre of a large estate which in the Dark Ages came down to the early Anglo-Saxon kings and was gifted (so later tradition said) to the bishopric of Winchester by King Cenwalh of the West Saxons in or soon after 634, at the time of his conversion to Christianity. From then on, with its rich medieval farming records and its diverse industries, the place is a mirror of English social history, aptly called here 'the town that became a village'.

The late great William Hoskins, who pioneered a new kind of English landscape history with *The Making of the English Landscape*, used to say that it ought to be possible to tell the story of the nation through any one place. This is certainly one of them. England is perhaps the best documented country in the world over the last thousand years; and Downton is one of a couple of hundred villages where the range and quantity of medieval manorial records allow a full portrait of village life over the centuries. Almost uniquely, Downton also has nearly thirty documents dating from the Anglo-Saxon period stretching back before the Norman Conquest to the 7th century. So Downton is one of only a handful of places where the story of the people could be attempted right across English history.

Foreword

In the Anglo-Saxon Age Downton was a thriving and populous estate whose people, largely unfree, gave their surplus to sustain the kingdom's most important bishopric. Its people saw the Viking wars close up, when fragmentary records from Winchester hint at the immense strains on life in places like Downton, of people ruined 'because of the stress caused by Viking raids'. A rare letter gives a vivid sense of life on one Winchester estate 'stripped bare by the heathen men.' Moving on to the eleventh century, the village was doing well. In the Domesday Survey of 1086 it had at least 600 people, perhaps more, with no less than seven mills; by the standards of the day almost a small town though that figure included the inhabitants of the dispersed farms and hamlets. After the Conquest it was important enough to have a Norman motte and bailey castle planted on the edge of the village. During the pre-Black Death boom time its population probably trebled, becoming a market town with 127 burgage plots, a fair, a market, a diversifying economy with weavers and a fulling mill for cloth production. But agriculture remained the chief occupation until the Napoleonic period, though from the 17th century tanning, then lacemaking, and later paper making, made their mark on its economy and landscape: as you go through Downton today you will still see the remains of small factories, mills and tanning works, along with some of the many Victorian pubs whose buildings survive today.

So the real-life Downton, today a thriving place of 3,000 people, is a place where the history of the nation can be read in miniature. It is full of fascinating stories, not least during the 1830s in the period of the rural riots of 'Captain Swing' when conditions became so bad that over 200 people were sponsored by the village to sail to Canada to make a new life the other side of the Atlantic: people whose descendants on the Great Lakes still cherish their links with old Wiltshire. In such tales Downton really is the British story in microcosm.

In his famous work of the 1960s, *The Making of the English Working Class,* E.P. Thompson spoke of his desire to rescue the poor Luddite weavers and framework knitters of the East Midlands from the 'enormous condescension of posterity', and that it seems to me is what local history does so effectively. This book shows that local history is also national history, and that national history is global history. It tells us who we are, how the community to which we belong was shaped by history and how our ordinary ancestors did much of the shaping. Local history is fascinating and illuminating and gives a great sense of empowerment, and all readers of this book I am sure, will be left with a strong sense of localism as they follow the village story. For after all, as the English writer, C. Henry Warren, put it in the middle of the Blitz: 'England is a Village'.

Preface

The village of Downton lies in the south-east corner of Wiltshire in the Avon valley below the plateau of the New Forest. It is a thriving community which has expanded rapidly since the end of the Second World War and its history is rich and varied. In 2004 I returned to Downton to live in the cottage in The Borough which had been my parents' and grandparents' home. I have known Downton all my life and had lived there briefly in my teens, though I had paid little attention to its history until moving into the village as an adult. My maternal grandfather, Bert Futcher, was a Downton man, and members of his family have lived for many generations in south Wiltshire. So when the opportunity arose to combine family history with a lifelong professional involvement with the past, an interest in my community became a passion to write the Downton story.

Downton is the largest village in Wiltshire and it may again become a town in the future so I shall start by explaining the title of this book. From 1395 until 1832 Downton was a borough[1] with the right to return two elected representatives to parliament. As a result of the Great Reform Act of 1832, Downton was disenfranchised and the borough was subsumed into the constituency of Wiltshire. Thus it lost the status of a small country town and for the purposes of government it reverted to being a village. It is this event which forms a central theme of the book.

This book is intended to be neither encyclopedic nor definitive. It draws on family, local and national history in an attempt to pull together previous work and to delve into areas where there has been no previous published research. It is not primarily a work of original research but it does contain some previously unpublished material. This is particularly the case with the sections on the Black Death and the Swing Riots. It is also an account of how major events in England's history have had an impact on the ordinary working people of this delightful corner of Wiltshire. It is this contextual view of local history that particularly interests me. Governed by the availability of sources, most history recounts the story of the minority of influential and powerful people and pays less attention to the majority of the population. I have attempted, where possible, to cover ordinary lives in Downton as well as the extraordinary.

The impact of both the internet and television has increased our interest in family history through local and genealogical research which are so closely related. That growth of interest has a bonus for, and puts a burden on, all local historians. A bonus for me because of the personal involvement by so many who have helped me with their own family stories and local knowledge; a burden because of the pressure to record accurately, even to the point of correcting previous accounts and debunking myths such as the Saxon origins of the Moot in Downton and King Arthur's association with Charford just a few miles to the south.

This book would not have been written without the support from family, friends, neighbours and professional historians whose names I record below. I begin with my late mother, who lived in Downton for the last thirty years of her life, though visited it from her early childhood. Her boxes of leaflets, books and photographs of the village formed the basis of my early research. She also recited to me stories about Downton, as did my grandparents. Secondly this book would not have been written without the support of a number of Downton residents. Of these I begin by thanking Margaret Smith who has proved to be a mine of information about the village, providing not only her personal memories of life in Downton since the Second World War but also sharing unselfishly her deep knowledge of local history and many old photographs. Also I am indebted to Margaret's son, Edward Green, for providing the inspiration to write an accurate and well-researched account, thanks to his excellent book, *Downton and the First World War*. My thanks are also due to Pat Cameron, Ann Ireland, Julia Whitmarsh, Don Moody, Bert Blake, Dennis Musslewhite, Les Ridgeley and Dr. Miranda Whitehead who have all been generous with their time and memories. I have also received support from Nicky Wilson, who was until recently the chair of the Downton Society and Ruth Webber, chair of Downton History Group. Jane and Peter Seden provided information on Downton productions and welcome hospitality whenever I needed to return to Downton. I must also thank Ken Light, a descendant of a Downton migrant to Canada, for the information provided on his website, and Carol Nelson for information on the Eastman family.

I would also like to express gratitude to a number of professional historians. I met Michael Wood, the historian and television presenter, at a charity event many years ago and one of our first topics of conversation was Downton, a village he knew through the study of

Anglo-Saxon documents. He followed up our conversation by sending me photocopies of several important references and guiding me in my initial research. At the time I was a busy teacher with no time to write a book but I was grateful to revisit his notes several years later and I also thank him for the foreword he has written for this book.

Dr. John Chandler has provided key guidance on writing local history and has advised on factual accuracy, and Dr John Elliott has advised on design, publication, religious topics and much else besides. Historian Martin Roberts' expertise in the nineteenth century and his honest and constructive feedback has been most welcome. Emeritus Professor David Hinton of Southampton University provided advice and material on the early medieval period. Professor John Morrill of Cambridge University, shared with me his research on the Monmouth rebellion in the seventeenth century. Dr. Rosalind Johnson of Winchester University provided me with information on non-conformism in Downton and Dr. Sean Lang of Anglia Ruskin University threw down the challenge to me that I should write this book in the first place.

I am grateful to the staff and archivists of the Wiltshire and Swindon History Centre, particularly Terry Bracher, for his advice on Wiltshire's rotten boroughs. The Hampshire Record Office at Winchester and the archivist at Winchester College have also offered advice and resources, as have Salisbury Museum, York Digital Archive and the Museum of Surfing. The Environment Agency provided advice, information and images on rivers and flooding. I also acknowledge a debt to David Waymouth who was courageous enough to attempt a full history of Downton in his book, *Downton, 7000 Years of an English Village*.

My two sons have also assisted in different ways; as a graduate geographer and environmentalist, Matthew Eaves provided me with information on river management and flooding in Downton. Peter Eaves translated from Latin a section of the 1349 Winchester Pipe Roll and advised me on several aspects of medieval history. This enabled me to include in the book previously unpublished data on the effects of the Black Death in Downton and information on the Moot. Finally my sincere and deep thanks go to my husband, Graham Hutchinson, who helped with research, proof read the book, took the present day photographs of the village, helped scan old photographs and generally put up with me spending long hours at the computer.

This book most certainly would not have been completed without them all.

Elizabeth Hutchinson
July 2015

An aerial view of Downton in the 1960s. From a postcard (Author's collection).

Introduction

On December 9th 2000, many people in Downton stood on the Iron Bridge over the River Avon, anxiously watching the rising waters. There had been several weeks of almost constant rain and Downton was on flood alert. The river, which usually provides beauty, pleasure and pride to this community in South Wiltshire, was about to burst its banks.

Downton was always particularly vulnerable to flooding. The rivers Nadder, Wylye, Ebble and Bourne all converge on the River Avon a few miles upstream from the village, and the combined force of five rivers then flows south through Downton, sweeping under Catherine Bridge which connects the upper and lower village. The present Catherine Bridge, also known as the Iron Bridge or County Bridge, was rebuilt in 1820. Its three arches span the river but also constrict the flow by obliging it to narrow slightly as it passes under the road. A wall of water, usually no more than a foot or two in height, often builds up on the upstream side of the bridge. On December 9th there was simply too much; the wall of water grew higher and more terrifying and as night fell water gradually spilled over the footpath which lies between The Borough and Catherine Meadow, into the cottages alongside it and then across the road and down the street. At about the same time the water level rose to the south of the bridge, and crept up the garden of the aptly named River Cottage.

Joan Gwyther, who lived in River Cottage, remembered the water first appearing in her kitchen, gently creeping under the doors on the ground floor of her 18th century cottage. She later described it in a letter to a friend in Australia.

> I was enjoying a nice fire and a good book, when I realised the ground floor was quietly filling with water. So with help from neighbours, it was chairs, tables, and whatever I could manage, up on bricks and now I'm writing this in my bedroom.

A postcard of Catherine Bridge, otherwise known as the Iron Bridge, in the early 20th century (Author's collection).

So it was with many other houses in the village. Everyone set to; neighbours helped each other and saved what they could. Precious possessions were carried upstairs, curtains were hitched up, rugs rolled and removed and furniture was lifted onto bricks in an attempt to minimise the damage. There was no panic, just a stalwart determination to do the best one could and to sit this one out. Floods had happened before, within the living memory of the older inhabitants, and they would get through this one again. Most people comforted themselves with the thought that in a few days the water would recede. When the level remained stubbornly high, local journalists and television crews arrived to record residents smiling and waving from upstairs windows along The Borough, shouting down to those in the street that they would stay put for now, their only complaint being that the speed of passing cars created a wash against their front doors.

The water did not recede for several weeks and most residents were eventually persuaded to leave their homes. It turned out to be the worst flood for 234 years. Forty properties were affected and a large number of residents had to be re-housed in temporary accommodation for months, not just until the water level went down, but until their houses dried out and remedial works were completed. The trauma was stoically borne and few complained. Flooding was a risk which most Downton people accepted. There had been very sizeable inundations recorded in 1606, 1631, 1636, 1795, 1883, 1915, 1954 and 1960, as well as many smaller occurrences. The River Avon is a central feature of the village. Occasional flooding, many said, was the price to be paid and as one wit stated, 'On a good day you're beside the river, on a bad day, you're in it!' In the new year of 2001 Downton mopped up and carried on.

Following this particular flood, Downton was designated by DEFRA as a special case and in 2003 an extensive flood defence scheme was designed and built, hopefully bringing to a close a recurring feature of Downton's history.

Most Downtonians would probably agree that the River Avon makes the village a special place. It attracted the very first inhabitants, many thousands of years ago. It has ever since provided livelihoods in agriculture and industry. It has given sustenance in the form of fish, wildfowl and water. It has given pleasure to fishermen, children, lovers of nature, swimmers and canoeists. It provides a home for mute swans, moorhens, kingfishers, ducks, otters, water voles and many other species. But it could bring discomfort and distress as well as pleasure so it is fitting that the river begins this story. It is the river and its periodic flooding which explain much in Downton's history.

Part 1

The River Avon, looking upstream towards New Court, with Clearbury Ring
clearly outlined on the horizon. From a 1960s calendar (Don Moody).

1

Early Settlement

The River Avon through Downton begins as two separate rivers, the western Avon and the eastern Avon. They merge near Upavon, flowing south across Salisbury Plain to Salisbury where the river is joined by the Nadder, the Wylye and the Bourne, then to the south of Salisbury, the Ebble. Thereafter it flows south along the western edge of the New Forest, through Downton to Fordingbridge and Ringwood and out into the sea at Christchurch Harbour. In ancient times the river was an east-west divide which was crossed at several fords along its length, including Downton, Britford, Longford and Charford.

To the west of the river the land rises gently to a height of 142 metres at Clearbury Ring and 114 metres at Gallows Hill, forming chalk outcrops, beneath which lie flat alluvium and gravel deposits of a valley about a kilometre in width. To the east the valley side is much closer to the river and the land rises more steeply to the plateau of the New Forest.[1] The fertile and attractive Avon valley attracted early man, Downton's first people, in the Old Stone Age or Palaeolithic era.

These first inhabitants left very scant remains because there were no permanent settlements. However an abundance of flint, still very evident today, particularly on the chalk downs north-east of Downton, provided useful raw material for primitive tools. Early hunter-gatherers were tool makers and flint tools served a variety of purposes including skinning, cutting and scraping of animal carcasses. Such tools have been discovered in Downton as well as in Woodgreen and Milford Hill. Many were found in the 1920s when one of the mills in Downton was converted into a hydro-electric power station. Some were kept

The chalk downs today, rising above Downton to the west of the River Avon.

in a glass-fronted case in the study of the headmaster, Mr. Scott, at the old secondary school in Gravel Close.[2] The mill in question has since been converted into a private house and straddles the Avon mill leat, opposite the aptly named Church Leat development.

The rich alluvial soil of the valley at Downton and the river attracted animals which were food for nomadic hunter gatherers. Prehistoric people followed their prey which came down from the higher ground to drink, hunting them for meat as well as gathering wild berries and seeds. These nomads, 'Homo Sapiens', who inhabited Britain it is believed for something like 700,000 years,[3] originally migrated out of Africa and thence across Europe into Britain at a time when the climate was colder, sea levels were lower and there was a land bridge between the British Isles and continental Europe.[4]

The earliest inhabitants for which we have evidence in the area we now know as Downton were prehistoric people who inhabited a simple shelter in the Mesolithic or Middle Stone Age. Excavations in Castle Meadow by Philip Rahtz in the 1950s revealed human settlement sometime between the third and fourth millennium BC. Although the extent of the occupation is uncertain, the site for this simple settlement appears to have been well-chosen as it was situated on a terrace just above the River Avon. It would have been free from flooding and yet close enough to the river to allow for a ready supply of water, fish, crustaceans and wildfowl. It is possible to surmise that the river might have been used for travel as well, at a time when the area was thickly forested and difficult to cross. Nearby there was a ready supply of flint. A 'chipping floor', where flints were worked into tools, was located during the excavation of the site and some 1,500 flint tools were found, including blades, scrapers and axes. A posthole was also found, suggesting a shelter was erected using either skins or reeds, supported by a single post.[5]

The site was probably used seasonally. These earliest of Downton settlers lived as semi-nomadic hunter-gatherers at the end of the last Ice Age and would have employed somewhat more sophisticated methods of hunting, fishing and trapping than their Paleolithic forebears. At times they would have moved on to new hunting grounds as they had not yet learnt how to exploit their environment as farmers.

Downton has also revealed Neolithic or New Stone Age remains from a period when hunter gatherers developed agricultural practices, growing crops and herding animals though still using stone tools.[6] The treeless chalk downs which can be seen above the Avon valley today are the result of clearances by Neolithic people. Previously these downs were thickly forested. Also to the west of Downton, on the downs rising from the Avon flood plain, there is a Neolithic long barrow or burial mound, known as the Giant's Grave, any bodies or artefacts long since stolen.

The Castle Meadow site which was excavated by Rahtz revealed evidence of habitation in the Neolithic or New Stone Age. Flint tools and sherds of pottery were unearthed but there was scant evidence of a settlement of any permanent nature. The flint tools included arrow heads, scrapers and a finely polished axe in mint condition. The pottery was of various types, some of it was identified by archaeologists as Beaker B ware, decorated in some cases with combs, cords and even fingers.[7]

The Giant's Chair, a Bronze Age round barrow to the west of Downton demonstrates the important development of metal working in the area and similarly lynchets or terraced fields at Standlynch date from this era. It was around 2,000BC that the Neolithic gave way to the Bronze Age in Britain. First gold and copper were worked and then bronze, a mixture of copper and tin. The art of metal working transformed society and probably bestowed great status and wealth on those who practised it. First emerging in the great civilisations of Mycenae and Crete, it may have been brought to Britain by the Beaker people who migrated from Europe. At about the same time the great monument of Stonehenge was being built and the Amesbury

The Giant's Grave (David Morgan).

Archer was buried. Members of his tribe may well have inhabited the Downton area as well.

The Amesbury Archer came from the Alps and archaeologists think he may have held a special place in society either because he was a metal worker or because he had a connection with Stonehenge. His grave, discovered less than twenty miles from Downton, is the richest prehistoric burial in Britain. It contained over 100 objects including copper knives, a tress of hair and beaker pots. Downton was situated within the area of the 'Wessex culture' which prehistorians and archaeologists agree was a place of special significance in prehistoric times.[8]

Two miles north west of Downton, clearly visible as a landmark for many miles around and identifiable by a copse of trees, is Clearbury Ring, an Iron Age hill fort. Situated at one of the highest points in the area it consists of a small enclosure defended by a bank and ditch. It was probably first constructed around 500 BC. By Iron Age standards it is quite small, occupying only about four acres. Not big enough to protect a large number of people and livestock permanently, it was most likely used for the shelter and protection of a minor chieftain. Having no water source, the nearest being the River Avon, it was probably only used as a defensive settlement in times of insecurity. Unfortunately any walkers who complete the upward trek to view it at close quarters will be confronted with a high fence and warnings to keep out.

Clearbury has never been excavated but the best evidence of the late prehistoric period lifestyle can be found at Danebury, near Winchester. Here an Iron Age hill fort was excavated by Professor Barry Cunliffe in the 1960s. Covering ten acres it was, according to

Cunliffe, essentially a military structure, with a complex gateway of banks and ditches to force attackers into a protracted approach. It was probably occupied by a chieftain and it provided protection and shelter for the tribe in times, which Cunliffe suggested, were essentially destabilised by warring factions. Although there are hill forts closer to Downton, the Danebury excavations undoubtedly provide the best evidence locally of Iron Age society, at a time which has left us no written records.[9]

To get a clearer account of these times we must turn to the Romans who wrote about our islands. It is fair to assume that by the first century before Christ, the Belgae, a confederation of tribes from northern France, Belgium, Holland and southern England were probably the dominant people inhabiting the Downton area and they were certainly well established by the time of Julius Caesar's unsuccessful invasions of Britain in 55 and 54 BC. Caesar's ambitions turned to Britain because the tribes in the south of the country had helped their Gallic kinsmen to resist Roman rule in Gaul. While Britain remained unconquered, Gaul was not securely under Roman control. Britain's

Clearbury Ring (Jim Champion).

The mosaic floor from the Roman villa at Downton (Salisbury Museum).

mineral wealth was also an attraction. Yet the land beyond Gaul across
the sea was regarded as uncivilised and many Romans doubted its
value. Although it was recognised that southern Britons were not as
wild or uncivilised as those in the north, Caesar later described the
Britons as having unkempt and facial hair and that they painted their
faces blue.[10] He also complained of miserable weather. The practice
of painting their bodies with woad is also attested by other Roman
authors including Ovid and Martial. A further insight into southern
British society at this time is provided by Tacitus, writing in the first
century AD. He described Britons as having a strong sense of fair play
and good governance and as spirited fighters, who used the chariot in
battle. He also commented that if it were not for inter-tribal rivalry
and fighting they would be a far more formidable opponent. He
writes of terrible weather too, 'the sky obscured by continual rain and
cloud', yet noting that the islands were perhaps worth the effort of
conquest due to a wealth of gold, silver and other metals.[11]

Caesar failed to establish a foothold in Britain in 55 and 54 BC but
it was eventually subjugated by the Roman emperor Claudius in an
invasion beginning in 43 AD. Hill forts held out against Roman armies
in many cases although there are no records of specific resistance by
Britons to Roman rule in the Avon valley. But when Roman armies

struck westwards from the Avon valley, there was certainly resistance. Archaeological excavations by Sir Mortimer Wheeler between 1934 and 1937 revealed signs of a bloody battle at Maiden Castle near Dorchester to resist the Roman army.

By no means all Britons opposed the government and influence of Rome. Realising the benefits of a more comfortable way of life in an empire which brought peace and trade, many soon aspired to the Roman way of life in the new Romano-British towns and villas.

Downton provides us with an insight into that way of life. Discovered in 1953 during the Moot Lane development, a fine, medium sized Roman villa was excavated in 1955-6.[12] It was later covered over when all items of interest and value had been removed from the site, so no trace of it can be seen today. It lies to the west of the old railway cutting, built on a terrace on the east side of the River Avon twenty feet above the normal river level, and comprised a central entrance, a front corridor and seven rooms in a line, one with a hypocaust, which had a stoke hole for heating the building. There was also a bath house and a corn-drying oven. It was a long narrow building facing west.

Lifting the mosaic from Downton Roman villa (University of York Dept. of Archaeology, and Estate of P. A. Rahtz).

The Downton villa bath house (University of York Dept. of Archaeology & Estate of P.A. Rahtz).

Building materials came from south Dorset and Somerset as well as the local area. It was dated to the period 250- 350 AD from 16 coins found on the site, including coins bearing the heads of Carausius and Licinius. Carausius was a Roman sea captain, who having cleared the North Sea of pirates, went on to declare himself emperor of Rome. He was murdered in 293 AD. Other finds included Samian ware pottery and animal bones of cattle, sheep, a small dog and a cat.

The most remarkable feature was a fine quality mosaic floor with a central motif of a cantharus, a Roman drinking cup, with two dolphin-shaped handles. This beautiful floor was chosen to be a centrepiece of the world class Wessex Gallery in the newly refurbished Salisbury Museum. It was almost certainly the floor of a dining room but, according to curator Adrian Green, was probably only used for about fifty years before the Roman empire collapsed.

The Downton villa was probably not the only building in the area. Very little of its rough flint outer walls survived. The footings and collapsed walls were discovered because of the extensive government

Opposite: Floor Plan of the Downton Roman Villa (Wiltshire Archaeological and Natural History Magazine and P. Rahtz).

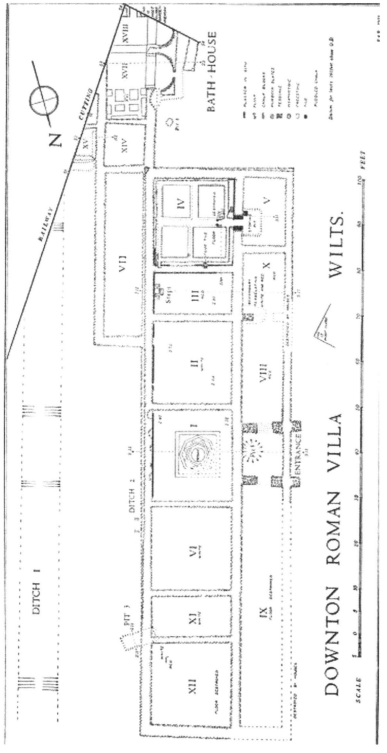

DOWNTON ROMAN VILLA WILTS.

house-building scheme shortly after the Second World War, when a resident of the Moot Lane development dug a hole for his washing line. After the removal of the mosaic floor the site was covered over again. To see a similar example one must visit Rockbourne a few miles south, to the west of the Avon. These two fine buildings attest to the fact that life in Romano-British villas would have been comfortable for the privileged few, though not for the majority. The owner of the Downton villa, who installed a smart new mosaic floor in his dining room, may just have witnessed a few years later the withdrawal of Roman rule from Britain in the early fifth century, although not the collapse of Roman life, which was much more gradual.

2

Unsettled Times

The Roman villa at Downton was occupied until at least the mid 4th century AD despite the fact that the stability and peace of the Roman empire had already been threatened by barbarian invasions late in the previous century. However when the Roman era drew to a close, local inhabitants would certainly have witnessed change. In Downton any potential danger may have seemed remote at first, and life in Roman Britain continued virtually unaffected for the time being. The inhabitants of southern and eastern Britain were generally well integrated into the civic and villa-based Roman ways, and may well have thought that such a life would carry on forever. The continuation of a gracious lifestyle in the Downton villa until at least the mid 4th century reflected this.

As the Roman occupation of Britain ended in the early 5th century, so the picture of life in the lower Avon valley becomes less clear. This is a period retrospectively named the Dark Ages. The Anglo Saxon Chronicle speaks of landings of Saxons along the south coast, although the archaeology does not reveal widespread evidence of Saxon occupation in much of the the Avon Valley until the 6th to 7th centuries. Anglo Saxon cemeteries with evidence dating from the later 5th to the early 6th century have been found to the north and south of Downton, and some of the pottery found in Downton's Romano-British villa in Moot Lane is of Saxon origin. Some of the latest pottery from the Moot Lane site could be as late as the 8th century. Its presence does not necessarily indicate continuous post- Roman habitation in Downton but it does show that some post-Roman inhabitants adopted a Saxon lifestyle at some point in this unsettled period.

Saxon pottery found on the site of the Roman villa at Downton (University of York Dept. of Archaeology & Estate of P. A. Rahtz).

Philip Rahtz suggested that the Roman villa at Downton was flourishing in the early 4th century, about 100 years before the collapse of the Roman empire. The latest Roman coin to have been found on the site was dated 330–335 AD. Rahtz surmised from this that the occupation of the villa by people who adopted a Roman lifestyle was in decline by the mid 4th century. One cannot assume that the occupants were Roman. They were more likely to to have been well-to-do Britons.[1]

'Britannia' formally ceased to be a Roman province in 410 AD when the Roman army was recalled to defend Rome against attacks by barbarian tribes. It was at this point that tribes from across the North Sea, Angles, Saxons and Jutes chiefly, were able to attack and occupy Britain.[2]

Exactly when and how did Saxon influence spread to this corner of south Wiltshire and what part did Downton play in the story? It is widely believed locally that a battle between Saxons and former inhabitants, the Britons, took place very close by at Charford. It is such an important aspect of local history, which has gathered some misunderstandings, that it is worth considering the evidence in detail.

The Saxon invaders consisted of scattered bands who were sporadically resisted by the native Britons. There was no organised invasion, nor any single authority on either side but resistance and conflict happened, much of it no doubt bloody. During the crisis

Ambrosius Aurelianus, a Romano-British aristocrat, made this appeal to Rome:

> I beg you to listen to the groans of the Britons, for the barbarians drive us into the sea and the sea drives us back to the barbarians.

His distress was understandable because Britain had enjoyed the benefits of Roman culture for four hundred years. Many leading Britons had adopted Roman life and the official religion of Christianity may well have taken hold quite extensively. The Saxons were different; they were pagan and they lacked an urban culture and infrastructure., So it is unsurprising that resistance to new Saxon settlements occurred, though the picture is confused by the lack of reliable written evidence. Myths and legends arose in the later Middle Ages,[3] compounded by the fact that in some cases the Britons employed Saxon mercenaries to defend their settlements.

The archaeology suggests that although the lower Avon valley stayed in British control for two centuries after the Roman legions left, the upper Avon valley fell to the Saxons sometime in the 5th century. This is at odds with an early version of the *Anglo Saxon Chronicle* which states that Cerdic and Cynric, who were two Anglo Saxon chieftains, landed on the south coast and headed north, defeating and killing the British king Natanleod, 'after whom the land up to Charford *(Cerdices Ford)* was called Netley,'[4] in 508 AD. One Downton legend suggested

The possible site of the Battle of Charford, photographed from Castle Hill, Woodgreen.

that Natanleod was buried in a tumulus which was levelled during the construction of the Moot ornamental garden between 1690 and 1705, but this folktale has no corroboration. It is more likely that, if a tumulus was levelled there at this time, it dated from the Bronze Age.[5]

A later version of the *Anglo Saxon Chronicle* (it went through several revisions) mentions a battle at 'Cerdices Ford' in 519 AD. A tenth-century version of the Chronicle by Aetheleard adds that this is 'by the Avon'. It is therefore tempting to identify the site as Charford, just south of Downton, particularly as the Domesday Book spelling of the settlement is *Cerdeford*.

In the 1930s the archaeologist O.G.S. Crawford suggested that Cerdic landed somewhere near what is now Totton. He claimed to have traced the route of the invading Saxons from the coast, via a path known as the Cloven Way, to Charford. In the vicinity of Downton, he suggested, this track runs from Cloven Hill in the New Forest, cutting across to Hatchett Green then via Home Farm, to a clearly visible cleft in the escarpment from the New Forest plateau down to Moot Lane and thence to a river crossing at Charford. The Ordnance Survey map still marks two fords, at North Charford and South Charford, each in turn taking the traveller from the east to the west bank of the Avon to join ancient trackways known as the North Charford Drove and the South Charford Drove. So the Cloven Way does seem to be a likely route for invaders landing near Southampton Water and then pressing north and west as they would have to cross the Avon at some point, although it must be stressed that there is no proof that the track in question was used for this purpose.

In 1894 the remains of an Anglo Saxon warrior were found on Witherington Down. Probably a man of substance, he was buried

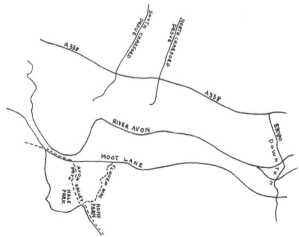

Map showing the location of the Cloven Way.

The Byzantine Bucket
found at Breamore
(Hampshire Cultural
Trust).

with a double-edged sword. Further evidence emerged more recently
when amateur archaeologist Steve Bulger, using a metal detector,
uncovered a 6th century Byzantine brass bucket. It was decorated
with a frieze of naked warriors fighting a leopard and another mythical
beast. An inscription running round the edge in Greek translates as,
'Use this, lady, for many happy years.' It was thought to have been
made in Antioch in what is now Turkey and was discovered in a field
at Shallows Farm, Breamore. This highly unusual find (there are only
twenty such buckets known to exist in the world) prompted Channel
4's Time Team to carry out a brief exploratory dig in the area. Eleven
early Saxon graves were found. In many ways this was not a typical
Anglo Saxon cemetery. There was a high ratio of weapons to burials,
eleven iron spearheads and nine shield bosses. Also found there
were six wooden buckets, encased in copper alloy, and a brass buckle
inset with red garnet and blue glass. The site was excavated under
time pressure on live television and clearly needs further work. It is
impossible to link the cemetery with certainty to any supposed battle
at Charford but its location is unusual, in a bend of the River Avon
on a peninsula of river gravel, as most cemeteries of this period were
on much higher ground. In a letter to the author, Professor David
Hinton of Southampton University suggested that the cemetery seems
to have been for a special group of people so that it could have been
remembered as a key place, and that the story of the battle of Cerdic's

Ford was told to explain the choice of location, rather than that the people in it had actually travelled and fought with the king.[6]

So it remains unproven that there was a battle fought for control of the Downton area and the Avon Valley at Charford, between native Britons and invading Saxons. Yet the archaeological and topographical evidence of the area to an extent ties in with the written evidence of the time that the invaders were struggling for control in the early 6th century. The observant walker travelling southwards out of Downton along Moot Lane will see land rising steeply from the Avon flood plain at Charford up to what is now the New Forest plateau, close to Castle Hill. The Cloven Way is clearly visible and exists as a byway from Home Farm to Moot Lane. Close by, below the escarpment, on the east side of the River Avon, there are also signs of additional banking and ditching which may date from this time but which have yet to be investigated. Was Downton very close to one of the most important battles of the early medieval period? Until more research is carried out there can be no definitive answer.

Inhabitants of the Downton area, such as they were at the time, may not have witnessed sudden changes despite the invasions from across the North Sea. The Roman way of life in Britain did not suddenly fall away or disappear completely. Rather, the majority of inhabitants continued to retain the Roman ways. There was a gradual disintegration of city life. Roads fell into disrepair but country life may have continued much as it always had. It was not until the late 6th century that Roman culture, civic organisation and security disappeared entirely, replaced by a country of tribal divisions and a more rural way of life.

One of the most noticeable changes in the area would have been the disintegration of organised Christianity. It had survived in pockets after the Romans armies left though by the 6th century its emphasis on personal worship and monasticism had resulted in doctrinal differences from Roman Catholicism. Christianity remained strongest on Britain's outlying fringes but was almost non-existent in Saxon strongholds, in effect most of what is now England. In the late 6th century Pope Gregory the Great dispatched Augustine to evangelise this former Roman province and to bring it into line with Roman Catholicism. Augustine landed in Kent in 597 AD and his influence led to the conversion of the Saxon King Aethelbert of Kent and later Edwin, King of Northumbria.

Downton was in the kingdom of the West Saxons or Wessex. There was no single nation or province of Britannia but instead a number of kingdoms. To return the people to the Christian fold the key was to baptise the king of each kingdom with the hope that his subjects would follow suit. In this way Christianity came to Wessex in 635 AD, when King Cynegils of the West Saxons was baptised, probably becoming the first Christian leader in the area since Roman times. He was converted to Christianity by the first bishop of the West Saxons, St. Birinus who allegedly came to Downton to re-establish a strong church. Birinus, a north Italian monk, was ordered by Pope Honorius I to spread the word of God in distant lands beyond England, presumably meaning Scotland. Having landed in Hampshire in 634 AD he decided to stay in the kingdom of the West Saxons to convert its heathen king and population, which duty he duly performed.[7] Birinus earned the title of the 'Apostle of Wessex' by converting its people and building churches, including laying the foundations of a church where Winchester cathedral now stands. He may have founded the church in Downton, but as is the case with many local stories, there is no hard evidence. His name is preserved in the church in neighbouring Redlynch but this has no factual or historical significance. After Cynegil's death, the new king of Wessex, Cenwalh, maintained Christian worship in the kingdom.

It was at this time that Downton developed as a village. The name Downton originates from 'Dunton', the Saxon word for 'farm by the downland'. It is mentioned in an Anglo Saxon charter of 672 AD although the authenticity and date of this charter is disputed. The name later goes through various spellings, Duntune, Duntone, Duneton and Donton to name a few. Of course it may have existed as a village in pre-Saxon times but there is no written record of earlier occupation. If there is any archaeological evidence, it lies beneath the modern village, almost certainly at the end near the church. This area is on higher ground away from the risk of flooding which was so much a feature on the west bank of the Avon.

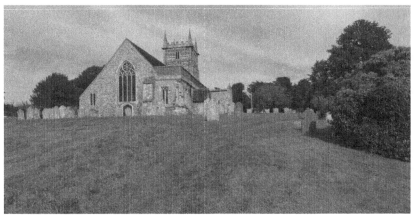

A view of St. Laurence Church, showing its prominent position on high ground.

Unsettled Times

The village of Downton in Saxon times would be almost unrecognisable today. The River Avon was probably forded, not bridged, and a muddy track would had led down from the forest plateau, possibly from Templeman's Farm and down Doctor's Alley to the river and up onto the downs to the west. There were no stone buildings. The parish church would have been a simple wooden structure, probably on or near its present position. One can imagine clusters of timber dwellings strung along the river valley, with walls infilled with cob, a mixture of sand, clay, water and organic material such as straw or horse hair. Roofs were thatched with local reeds or straw. Gravel was probably extracted from the river bed to provide track infill and hut foundations. Perhaps the name 'Gravel Close' came from such practices. Poorer families almost certainly shared accommodation with livestock in winter, not just to house the livestock but also to provide body heat in cold weather. Privacy was something completely unknown even for the wealthy. Eating and sleeping together in one room was the norm, whether it was a peasant family in a hut or a noble family in a great hall. Life expectancy was probably not much more than half what it is today. Hunger and disease were ever present dangers, even though this was a pleasant and fertile valley.

Society was very different too. Saxon society dictated that land was held in return for military service. This bound men together, peasants to overlords and lords to kings. It was a society based on war and plunder as well as on loyalty and honour. Blood feuds, whereby damage to a person should be avenged, and wergild, a system which dictated that every crime had a price to be exacted by the victim or his supporters, meant that it was the family and the tribe which dealt justice on an unforgiving basis. This contrasted with Christian teachings and conversion to Christianity necessitated adopting new kinds of societal interaction.

It used to be thought that the Downton Moot was a Saxon meeting place and a site of local government and jurisdiction. For example an article in *Country Life* published in 1909 stated;

> There seems no doubt about it that the terraced steep in Mr. Squarey's charming grounds at Downton is a surviving parliament place of Saxon times.[8]

Mr Squarey mentioned here was Elias Pitt Squarey, the owner of Moot House in the early 20th century. Clearly in no hurry to play down the historical importance of his beautiful garden, still known as the Moot, he later repeated the claim in a booklet which he wrote about his property.[9] We now know that the earthwork mentioned in

The Moot gardens in the early part of the 20th century, from a postcard (Margaret Smith).

both publications dates from a later age which is dealt with in the next chapter. However the area immediately south of the Moot has yielded evidence of Saxon occupation from the 7th to 8th centuries. The archaeologist Philip Rahtz excavated a Saxon gravel pit at about the same time as he completed his Roman excavations. Rahtz suggested that the gravel was extracted by Saxon villagers to use as foundation material for buildings constructed on the flood plain, possibly underneath the present houses of Downton. The pottery he found is of a simple hand-made type, coloured black, and finds included an early medieval cooking pot and various sherds. They were not really dateable. Once the gravel had been extracted, the pit was used for domestic rubbish.[10]

The gravel pit in question lies south of substantial Saxon foundations, first noticed by the pioneering archaeologist, General Pitt-Rivers, in the nineteenth century. These foundations, known locally as 'Old Court' or the 'Bishop's Palace' lie beneath the ground on what is now an island in the River Avon to the west of the Moot monument. In Saxon times this was not an island but was part of the east bank, The mill leet was later cut through to create the island we see today. The building may have been used by the bishop of Winchester when he visited Downton, although a more likely location for his Downton residence would have been on higher ground in the vicinity of the church as the island is vulnerable to flooding.

In Saxon times the history of Downton became linked with Winchester when the village and surrounding farmland, known as

Downton Mills. The possible site of the Bishop's Palace is on the island in the right foreground. In the background, St. Laurence Church tower and the Tannery building.

an estate, was granted to the bishopric of Winchester. Exactly when this happened is a matter of debate. There exists an undated Saxon charter in which Cenwalh, King of the West Saxons from 643 AD to 672 AD gave 100 'mansae' in Downton to the church of St. Peter and St. Paul in Winchester. However H.P.R. Finberg, an eminent scholar of the Saxon period, suggested the charter was a forgery, written in the reign of King Offa of Mercia (757-796 AD), and that Offa himself was responsible for the gift of Downton to Winchester. Finberg argued that Cenwalh's name was inserted in the charter to give it greater validity.[11]

Whichever theory is followed, 796 AD is the latest date for the gift of Downton to the see of Winchester. The fact that the village was settled as a gift from a king to one of his highest ranking churchmen in the land makes it a fair assumption that by the late 8th century Downton was a substantial settlement and a rich estate. The 100 mansae referred to in the charters was greater area than the village of Downton and probably consisted of a continuous tract of land between the Avon valley and the Ebble valley.[12] It became a valuable and important part of the estate of the bishop of Winchester and the income from Downton contributed considerably to the Bishop's wealth. Bishops of Winchester were among the most powerful men not just in England but in Europe.

Successive bishops visited Downton from time to time and for this they required a substantial residence in the village, befitting an important prelate of the church for, despite the lack of good roads, regular checks on their estates were vital. The likely route from Winchester to Downton was by a track south of the Clarendon Way which follows the ridge from Dean Hill to Pepperbox Hill and then south to the modern day Templeman's Farm.[13] Following high ground in this way avoided the inherent dangers of crossing the plateau of what is now the New Forest, a sparsely populated wilderness. Downton was also situated on the route from Winchester to Hindon, another of the bishops' possessions. Part of this route was known in Saxon times as Hedda's Grove or Grave, supposedly after the fifth bishop of Winchester, Hedda, who died in 705 AD. Bede in his *Ecclesiastical History of Britain* records him as a 'good and just man (who) exercised his episcopal duties rather by his innate love of virtue than by what he had gained by learning.' David Waymouth asserts that he died in Downton and was buried at Pepperbox but there is no evidence for this and it seems unlikely, particularly as his remains were later associated with miracles at Winchester, suggesting that his burial was there.[14]

At least nine Anglo Saxon charters refer to Downton, a rich cache of written documents for a settlement of this size. Five of the charters were rediscovered in the early 20th century. They had been copied into a 12th century cartulary (a collection of documents) made by the monks of St. Swithun's Priory, Winchester, and this ancient volume was discovered to have been propping up a small chorister's seat in the early 20th century. The charters referring to Downton were studied by Revd. A. Du Boulay Hill who at the time was the vicar of Downton.[15] They reveal that from time to time Downton was seized back from the church by a Wessex king only to be later returned to the bishopric. The first undated, possibly forged charter is the grant of Downton to Winchester by King Cenwahl. The second refers to a restitution by King Egbert in 826 AD. This is confirmed in a third charter in the reign of King Athelstan in 932 AD. The fourth grants another restitution by King Eadred in 948 AD and the fifth confirms the grant by King Ethelred shortly before the Norman Conquest. It was not uncommon in Saxon times for kings to seize church land and give it to retainers in return for a lifetime of loyal service. When the retainer died the king or his heir might return the land to the church, as it was thought that in this way he might save his soul. The seizure of church lands and their subsequent return may seem a somewhat irresponsible and unholy way to conduct themselves but this was an age when the Anglo Saxons were not fully committed to Christianity. Elements of paganism and old ways still persisted.[16]

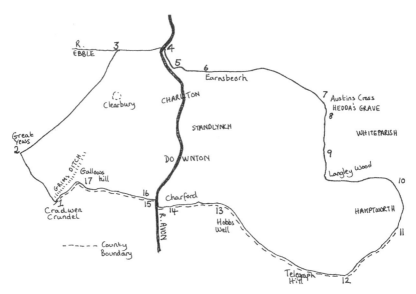

A sketch map showing Downton's Anglo-Saxon boundaries (after Du Boulay Hill).

A further reference to Downton appears in the will of King Eadred in 997 AD when he bequeathed the villages of Downton, Damerham and Calne to Winchester, clearly showing that at that time Downton was back in royal rather than church hands.

In the later charters the boundaries of the manor of Downton were clearly defined in writing though they were not mapped at the time. They appear to have remained unaltered throughout the Saxon period. Revd. Du Boulay Hill traced the landmarks defining these boundaries on the ground and discovered that in a remarkable example of continuity they almost coincide with parish boundaries as shown in the tithe map of 1841. Thus the Saxon boundaries of Downton were described as follows. The numbering, mapping and modern definitions are Du Boulay Hill's.

First from Cradwen Crundel, Number 1, This may refer to a marker stone near the end of Grim's Ditch as it touches Cawdon Hundred.

To Warriors Hill, to the ford's meadow, to Ebbesbourne at Afen. This is north-west from Cradwen Crundel to Great Yews, number 2 on the map, then north-east between Odstock and Nunton churches, crossing the River Ebble, number 3, and following it to the junction with the Avon at number 4.

To the Vetches, to the Mudeley Lake. The boundary turns south along the Avon at Bodenham and departs from the river at number 5.

To Eornsbeorh. The boundary rises east from the river, traverses Witherington Ring and the old stockaded entrenchments called the Lynchetts, by an old road known as Pack Path. The earthwork may be 'Earnsbeorh' at number 6.

To a ditch at Bered's Tree, to the warpath, to Hedda's Grave. The boundary reaches the top of the down, turns and strikes the Salisbury-Whiteparish road then heads east for half a mile along the road to Pepperbox at number 7.

Then along the hedge at Witan Wyrth to Water Brook to Willow. Witan Wyrth means Counsellor's or Council Field, which Hill noted still bore the same name. From there the boundary follows a line of yew trees, number 8, running south and continues to New House, number 9, and Langley Wood.

To the ditch at Hiceles Wyrth. It turns and runs east for about two miles to Langley Bridge, number 10.

Then across the open field to the hedge out through Brember Wood to the Stone Post. Numbers 11 and 12.

Along the warpath to Fobb's Spring. Number 13. These last two follow the county boundary. Hill found a spring still known as Hobb's Well.

Along the warpath to the hedge end and fair battle ford. Numbers 14-15. Is the memory of a battle at Charford still echoed here as the boundary strikes the Avon again at right angles?

And finally, **to the hedge, to Ceorles Hlawe.** This is identified as Gallows Hill, number 17.

Thus du Boulay Hill found some intriguing continuities between Saxon and modern Downton, in terms of place names and boundaries.

By the 9th century the bishops of Winchester were the undisputed overlords of Downton. The village formed a valuable manor of an important man. Whoever held the bishopric was influential and close to the king because Winchester had been the capital of the West Saxons since about 686 AD.

Unsettled Times

The Vikings

After many years of relative peace and security, the area was threatened in the late 8th century by another wave of invaders and Downton may well have experienced something of the conflict. The first attacks of the Vikings who originated from areas of Scandinavia, including Norway and Denmark, were initially successful in the north of England. In 860 AD they sacked Winchester. By 865 AD the Anglo Saxon Northumbrian kingdom fell to the invaders and by 870 AD Vikings from the area now occupied by Denmark were in the Thames valley. They were a direct threat to Wessex again and to Downton, The fate of the kingdom of Wessex lay in the hands of two brothers of the royal house of Wessex, Alfred and Aethelred, who fought a series of battles against them in 871 AD. Following Aethelred's death, it was left to King Alfred alone to defend the region. In 878 AD after a surprise attack by the Danes on Chippenham. Alfred pulled together a Saxon army and won a great victory. This made Alfred the most powerful leader in England, and as Winchester was the capital of Wessex it was one of most the important cities in the land. Downton lay at the heart of Wessex and, given that there was a strong Viking presence to the south, in and around Poole harbour, and in the north, around Chippenham, it can be surmised that the invaders were probably in the Downton area at some point. This is supported by the discovery of three iron axes in 1930 during building work on Mill Bridge. The axes were examined by the celebrated archaeologist, Sir Mortimer Wheeler, two being identified as Saxon and one Viking, perhaps the spoils of war.

Yet, in the words of Simon Schama:

> peasants (unfree tenants or serfs) ploughed their fields, fed swill to their pigs, prayed to avoid poverty and pestilence and watched the seasons roll round.[17]

The momentous events affecting the royal house of Wessex may have barely touched most inhabitants of Downton and even the subsequent conquest of the kingdom by the Danish Cnut in 1016 may have passed almost unnoticed, particularly as Cnut recognised the wisdom of preserving well-established Saxon institutions. To what extent lives were affected by the Norman conquest of 1066 is a question for the next chapter.

3

New Masters

Downton was a well-established community by the time William of Normandy claimed the English throne in 1066. The village gave its name to the 'Downton Hundred' which was a division of land first used by the Anglo Saxons. In theory a hundred contained 100 hides and a hide was enough land to support one extended family. The name Hyde Lane in Downton probably originates from the term. The Downton Hundred consisted of not just the village but also the parishes of Hindon, Bishop's Fonthill, Bishopstone, Bodenham and Nunton, East Knoyle and Standlynch.

In the 11th century the surrounding land was farmed as arable and pasture, with the emphasis on arable increasing during the Saxon period. The field systems can still be seen on high ground above the river valley particularly at Wick (itself a Saxon word for a hamlet). Agricultural practices which were to continue for many hundreds of years were probably well established by this time; sheep were grazed on the downs rising above the river valley and were brought down to the lower ground to provide manure for improving and fertilising the soil from time to time. Arable land was divided into strips, with unploughed grass boundaries between each strip. The soil would have been wetter than today; flooding of the river was more frequent as the land did not benefit from drainage schemes. The thinner soils and lack of water on the higher ground meant that settlement was strung along the river valley with its good arable soils and accessible water supply.[1] No further expansion occurred on higher ground until the late Middle Ages.

Exactly how the Norman conquest affected Downton is difficult to judge, although we know that the manor of Downton was confirmed

Hyde Lane at the turn of the 20th century (Margaret Smith).

as part of the estate of the bishop of Winchester after the conquest. Wakelin, a nominee of William the Conqueror and a member of his family, was awarded the Winchester bishopric and its estates, including Downton. It is unlikely that Downton's ordinary inhabitants were immediately aware of the great or sudden political change that had taken place even though the old Anglo Saxon ruling classes were mostly displaced by the conquest. If any Anglo Saxon aristocrats had survived either the three battles in 1066, the rising in the north in 1069 or local rebellions such as the one near Ely led by Hereward the Wake, they were, with few exceptions, dispossessed or replaced by Normans loyal to William. Although Wessex was relatively subdued by comparison, by 1086 only two out of 1,400 tenants-in-chief to the Crown in England were of Anglo Saxon origin, the rest were Norman retainers whom William I rewarded with gifts of land and titles. The new Norman king kept a firm grip on his newly conquered realm.

The Domesday Book, which was compiled for William I in 1086 as a tax assessment, lists Downton as Duntone and recites that there were then seven mills and fifty-nine and a half hides on the estate. The land was a mixture of arable, meadow, woodland and pasture. There were sixty-four villagers, twenty-seven smallholders and forty slaves accounted for. However it is important to remember that not all of this necessarily relates to the village of Downton as we know it today as it also included some possessions in surrounding areas.[2] Neither can Domesday provide us with an accurate population figure as it was compiled for fiscal purposes only, although the total population has been estimated at around 650 people.[3]

It is fair to say that the conquered Anglo Saxons including the people of Downton were viewed as second class citizens. There developed a sharp social divide with little intermarriage between the Norman nobility and the conquered lower classes for at least two centuries. French was the language of the rulers and it remained so until the Hundred Years War in the 14th and 15th centuries. The Anglo Saxon language was the vernacular of the lower classes; it was the language of farming, trade and everyday life and would continue to be spoken in Downton. Many of the old words remain in use today, illustrating the social division between those who produced and those who consumed, thus for example the word 'cow', an Anglo Saxon word, continued to be used by the labourers who reared them, while 'beef', a French word in origin, was for the Normans who consumed. One element of continuity was that the Normans carried over from their predecessors the social and governmental system of feudalism with its obligation of service to the lord or, in the case of tenants-in-chief, to the king in return for security and property, but these obligations were made much clearer than in Anglo Saxon times.

Early Norman influence is no longer apparent in Downton but is most visible at Old Sarum. Lying approximately eight miles north of Downton, it was here that William the Conqueror was presented with the Domesday Book. William had fortified the earthwork as an army base during the early stages of the Norman conquest. Although there is little evidence of occupation at Old Sarum in the late Saxon period the Normans threw up an impressive motte inside the ancient hill fort and built a number of towers, halls and apartments.[4] It also became the site of a new cathedral.

Plans for the Old Sarum cathedral originated after the Council of London in 1075, where it was decreed that the Sherborne bishopric should be transferred to Old Sarum. The bishop at the time was Herman, but the major work was completed under his successor,

Osmund (1078–99) who shaped the character and constitution of Old Sarum Cathedral. The creation of Old Sarum as a religious centre of power led to the anomaly that Downton fell into the diocese of Salisbury while its feudal obligations remained with Winchester. To acknowledge this fact, the rector of Downton, a Winchester appointee, paid half a mark annually to the bishop of Old Sarum, and latterly New Sarum or Salisbury, from the tithes he collected from the villagers of Downton. The considerable profits from the manor of Downton to the bishop of Winchester helped pay for the building of a magnificent new Norman cathedral at Winchester, ordered by Wakelin and completed in 1079. Downton was by this time the second largest manorial estate of the bishopric of Winchester after Taunton. Three-quarters of the estate was tenanted and the rest directly controlled and farmed by officials of the lord bishop. In medieval times land farmed directly by the lord of the manor or his agents was known as demesne land.

Close to Downton King William established a new hunting ground, Nova Foresta, or the New Forest in 1079. Later medieval chroniclers criticised King William I for expelling people from their homes to create his private hunting ground, even suggesting that the death of his son, William Rufus, in the New Forest, was a kind of divine retribution for these land clearances.[5] William I imposed strict and widely detested laws on the sparsely populated area in order to encourage and conserve deer and wild boar and to prevent poaching. The fencing of land was prohibited in case it interfered with the chase and game was considered more valuable than a man's life. Where the laws were flouted punishment was mutilation or death. As for William Rufus, the debate continues about whether the arrow which killed him was fired accidentally or deliberately. His body was carried back to Winchester Cathedral where it still lies.

The village of Downton lies just outside the forest boundary, but it was later reported that there were 'two hides from which the villagers have fled because of the King's forest'.[6] The village was also likely to have been affected in other ways. For medieval kings, hunting was not just an amusing hobby, it provided vital training in horsemanship and weaponry. For William I and his successors it was important time spent in the New Forest and so it is likely that the area was often graced with a royal presence. As all feudal landholding was by grace of the monarch, the bishop of Winchester would have been duty bound to provide provisions for royal banquets when kings were close at hand. Downton would have been expected to supply local produce for the royal table.

The Moot

Today the Moot Garden is a scheduled ancient monument and a venue for local activities. In the Middle Ages it became a symbol of royal power. Saved from neglect and decay by the Downton Moot Preservation Trust, formed in 1987, the gardens nowadays provide a delightful leisure facility and entertainment space. In the 12th century the Moot was constructed as a defensive castle. The site has been largely misunderstood until recent times; it had been thought that the sunken lawn within the Moot area with its grassy amphitheatre and raised central area was a Saxon meeting place or moot, hence the more recent name. Shire and hundred moots did exist in Saxon times, their purpose being to discuss local issues and they were attended by local lords and bishops as well as representatives from the village.[7] Moots should not be confused with Witans which were convened by the king and which were precursors of our modern parliament. However the Downton Moot served neither function. One clue lies in its location because Saxon Moots were almost always located at the junction of important tracks or roads and on high ground, so that they could be easily found, the spot often being simply marked by an oak tree. This is not the case in Downton.

Although there was almost certainly an earlier settlement there, the Downton Moot's place in history lies in the 12th century and it is closely linked with an important national event. It was built as a motte and bailey castle to guard the river crossing during the civil war between Stephen and Matilda. Orders for the construction of the

An early photograph of the Moot gardens. The pond and the summer house formed part of the 18th-century landscaping of the Norman castle. (Margaret Smith).

The sundial lawn in the centre of the Moot bailey. The presence of the raised area in the centre may have led to its misinterpretation as a Saxon meeting place (Margaret Smith).

castle were given by Henry of Blois, a maternal grandson of William the Conqueror and first cousin of Matilda, the daughter of King Henry I of England, who was appointed bishop of Winchester in 1129. He was a talented administrator and an influential and powerful man of his time. His main residence was Winchester Palace in London, the remains of which can still be seen on the South Bank. He channelled considerable profits from his estates, including Downton, into embellishing Winchester Palace in London and Winchester Cathedral and commissioned some of the finest manuscripts produced by the monks of Winchester.[8]

In order to support his brother Stephen's claim to the throne of England, in 1138 Henry of Blois built or strengthened castles at Downton, Taunton, Farnham, Waltham and Merdon. In Downton this was when the earthen mound or motte and outer bailey or courtyard were raised. There is no evidence of any stonework, the presumption being that it simply comprised a timber stockade surmounting the motte which was positioned within a fenced bailey or courtyard. The earthworks are nevertheless impressive and are possibly one of the largest ringworks of the time in England.[9] The motte or central mound is still clearly visible behind the Waterside cottages but only a fraction of the bank of the outer bailey is now visible to the south of the present entrance because the line of the bailey extends underneath the present day High Street and beneath the Tannery House and garden. In 1991 a small excavation by

Professor David Hinton of Southampton University revealed pottery sherds of Roman origin and some of Saxon and Medieval provenance, possibly from the 12th century. The absence of masonry suggests that stone fortifications were never built. It is more likely that the Bishop's Palace situated on the east bank of the Avon adjacent to the Moot, was fortified.[10] This palace may have been part of the same complex, using the Moot for security.

Henry of Blois built the castle at Downton when England was experiencing uncertain times; a contest between two rival claimants to the throne of England. This arose when in 1120 the 'White Ship' went down in the English Channel, carrying with it Prince William, the sole surviving legitimate son of Henry I. When Henry I died in 1135 his daughter Matilda was the first in line to the throne, which was also claimed by her cousin Stephen, the son of William the Conqueror's daughter Adele and brother of Henry of Blois, the Bishop of Winchester. As a result England entered, in the words of the Anglo Saxon Chronicle:

> a time of war ... every great man built himself castles and held them against the king ... they sorely burdened the unhappy people of the country with forced labour.

The chronicle goes on to describe atrocities:

Mill Bridge Downton.

An old photograph taken of Mill Bridge with the raised mound of the Moot behind. The trees in the background on the higher ground are growing on top of the motte of Henry of Blois' fortification. Most of these trees were blown down in the great storm of 1987 (Margaret Smith)..

when the wretched people had no more to give, they plundered
and burned all the villages ... the wretched people perished with
hunger ... never did a country endure greater misery.

In the proximity of Downton were the armies of the two rival
factions and the village was on the front line. To the west lay territory
controlled by Henry of Blois, supporting Stephen, and to the east
lay Salisbury, Christchurch and Ludgershall, strongholds supporting
Matilda. The defence of Stephen's claim was very much in the hands
of his brother while Stephen himself was fighting near Oxford and
London. Downton became a vital stronghold for Stephen. In 1148
Earl Patrick of Salisbury, supporting Matilda, seized Downton Castle
and used it as a base to launch raids into Hampshire. Henry of Blois
gave his nephew Hugh de Puiset the task of recapturing Downton.
De Puiset built a seige engine with which he managed to recapture
the castle.[11] Although there is no written or archaeological evidence
as to how long the battle to recapture the castle took, it seems likely
that the *Anglo Saxon Chronicle* description of the civil war between
Stephen and Matilda aptly recounts the experience of Downton's
inhabitants. It is known that Stephen felt betrayed by Salisbury's
loyalty to Matilda and his brother Henry may well have taken his
revenge on traitors locally.

A year later Matilda reluctantly gave up her claim to the English
throne and she returned to the continent. The war ended in 1153

An early 20th century photograph of the Moot, during a fete. It clearly shows
the bailey, or outer ringwork (Margaret Smith).

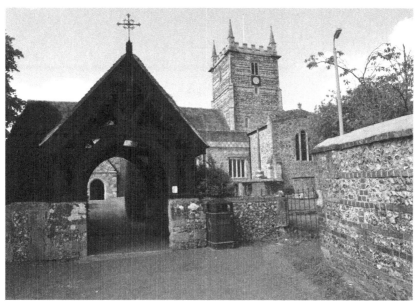

St.Laurence church.

when a formal compromise was reached whereby Stephen was recognised as king for the rest of his life and would be succeeded by Matilda's son, the future Henry II. In 1154 Stephen died, and Henry II became King of England.

Despite these violent times the castle at Downton was never fortified in stone. This may have been due to lack of money but a more likely explanation, given that Downton was a rich estate, is that it was the result of Henry II's policy of a nationwide crackdown on unlicensed castles in an attempt to bring law and order to England after the anarchy of Stephen's reign.

The castle was probably destroyed in 1155, at which point the outer bailey ditch was filled in. A small trial excavation in 1990 revealed a sherd of 12th century pottery of an unglazed coarse sandy clay which was common in this area. Its discovery accords with the date of the castle's destruction. The destruction is also recited in the Chronicle of Robert Torigny.[13]

The initial phase of construction of the present parish church of St. Laurence also dates from this time. The earliest visible parts, the first three arches of the nave, date from 1130-50. It was probably also the work of Henry of Blois but unlike the Moot it heralded times of greater peace and stability. This was true not just of Downton but of the country as a whole. After a bloody civil war it seemed that finally Downton was set for a turn of fortune.

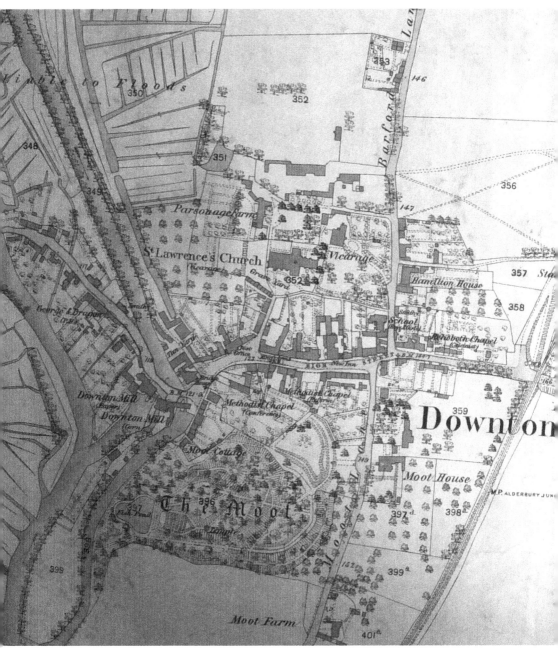

A section of the 1876 Ordnance Survey map of Downton, showing the upper part of the village. The image is taken from the Women's Institute Scrapbook of Downton which was compiled in 1956.

4

The Borough of Downton

Downton experienced one of the most important turning points in its history in the 13th century when the village was transformed into a market town. In 1208-9, twenty years after the death of Henry II, the new bishop of Winchester, Peter des Roches, radically changed its character and raised its status by creating the borough of Downton.[1]

Des Roches sought to increase the revenue from his estates by developing six of the Winchester manors into new towns.[2] In Downton, this entailed extending the area of settlement to the west side of the River Avon. The original village was adjacent to the parish church east of the river. To the west a broad street was now laid out, flanked on both sides by cottages each of which had long garden plots behind them. The street still bears the name, 'The Borough'[3] and the pattern of housing is preserved. Most inhabitants of the bishop's manor of Downton remained unfree peasants under feudal obligations but tenants in the new borough would be rent-paying free citizens. They did not have the restrictions which were imposed on manorial peasants and they could engage in their own trades, although the bishop's court still retained the right to settle disputes, oversee transactions and regulate fairs and markets.

In Downton the properties in the bishop's borough were set out so that the new street would allow space for markets and fairs along its length. It ran parallel to and slightly south of the old road from Doctor's Alley to Wick Lane, nowadays known at its western end as Long Close. The new site may have been chosen to take advantage of a slightly higher ridge of land running east to west to avoid the risk of flooding. Today the modern road runs along the northern side of this area and is flanked to the south by three large village greens. In the

The effigy of Bishop Peter des Roches in Winchester Cathedral
(Prof. Nicholas Vincent, UEA).

13th century there was unlikely to have been a distinction between road and green, instead the whole of The Borough formed a wide open space, earthen and dusty in the summer, muddy in the winter.

There are no buildings in Downton still standing which date from the foundation of the borough but most old properties in the street called The Borough probably rest on the footprints of dwellings established in the 13th century. Each burgage property consisted of a cottage fronting the street with a lengthy plot to the rear for vegetables, poultry and maybe pigs. The layout of these cottages and plots remains largely unchanged to this day, except some burgage properties have been split in two, such as the former number 87, now 112 and 114 The Borough. Unfortunately several old cottages were demolished and replaced by new properties in the 1960s and most of these are sited further back from The Borough than the original burgage properties.

The bishop benefited in numerous ways from this arrangement. He remained a feudal lord of the old manor of Downton, producing agricultural produce from his own demesne lands, and he now had a convenient market centre in which to sell produce. In addition, by attracting stall holders and traders to Downton he ensured that he had access to a variety of goods to satisfy his tastes when he visited. The charge to stallholders increased his income and no doubt he hoped that the Downton borough would develop because the 13th century

The Borough, wide enough to allow space for markets and fairs. The contrast with the narrowness of the old High Street is apparent (Margaret Smith).

was a time of population growth, improved weather conditions and economic expansion, with large scale sheep farming a significant feature of agriculture on his estate. Downton was by no means unique, as Des Roches developed five other boroughs on his estates in the

This old photograph shows cottages in The Borough before tarmac was laid, giving a hint of its appearance in the 13th century. The cottages in the foreground are of a similar construction to dwellings of medieval times (Margaret Smith).

This photograph was taken for a calendar in the 1950s. It shows the long back garden of 'Stubby' Sherwood with a pigsty (Don Moody).

South-West and this was not unusual, as lords of manors were creating new market towns all over the country at this time.

The Downton market developed quickly at first. In 1208-9 19 stall holders paid rent and by 1213-14 there were 72 stall holders. As for the new burgage plots, there were 89 tenants paying rent by 1218-19, two of whom were weavers; a fulling mill in the village paid 40 shillings rent which equated to approximately half of all the burgage rents combined. The presence of weavers and a fulling mill indicate that wool was traded in the new market town. In the early 13th century wool was more likely to have been sold on to the local woollen manufacturing industry rather than being exported.

Tenants in the borough or burgesses paid the bishop one shilling a year rent. In 1275 Edward I summoned nobles and churchmen to attend a parliament and he also issued orders known as writs for the election of two representatives from each county (the knights of the shire) and two from each borough (the burgesses). Thus originated the right of Downton to send two burgesses to parliament. This right to vote would later, although not immediately, become important as members of parliament did not begin to influence policy until the late 17th century.

Eventually properties had a burgage number painted on the front wall as evidence that the tenants or owners had a right to vote. Only

Creel Cottage displaying its burgage number.

one such painted number remains today, on Creel Cottage next to the River Avon. No doubt the tenant painted his number very large to ensure everyone knew he had the right to vote and this may have been a common practice. Burgage numbers can also still be seen on other properties carved in stone blocks set in the masonry. These do not date from the foundation of the borough but were put in place in the 18th century to prevent fraud.

An 18th-century stone burgage number.

The Borough of Downton

Old and traditional ways continued in the manor of Downton which co-existed with the new borough, so that manorial tenants did not have voting rights, neither did they pay rent but they provided labour services, in other words they performed specific work in return for their cottages and smallholdings. Arable land was mainly situated in three enormous open fields which in turn were divided into blocks known as furlongs. Furlongs were sub-divided into strips with grass baulks between them. In the three field system the manor regulated the crop rotation whereby each field lay fallow every three years. This meant that yields were low and hunger was common. Hunting and fishing, which could supplement a poor diet, were strictly controlled under the manorial system. Manorial customary tenants also had rights of pasture for their animals, but there was only limited winter fodder so many animals had to be slaughtered in the autumn and the meat salted to preserve it through the winter. Awareness of selective breeding of livestock was rudimentary. Farm animals of today, the product of centuries of selective breeding, look very different from their puny medieval ancestors.

The demesne lands farmed with labour services on behalf of the lord bishop lay mainly in the Wick area. This fact may explain the name of the Headlands, a stretch of the modern A338 road. In medieval times the term headland referred to the land at the end of the cultivated strips which allowed draught animals to turn when ploughing. Direct cultivation of the demesne land was at a high point in 1208-9, after which records show the Lord Bishop was letting out

The pound was situated opposite the present day Memorial Hall within living memory (Margaret Smith).

more land to tenants, a decision which, in Downton, coincides with the foundation of the borough.

The open fields vanished with little trace in later centuries, though one remnant of the medieval farming system survived in Downton until the 20th century and that was the role of the hayward who ensured animals did not stray onto arable fields which were unfenced and unhedged. In most parts of England, when fields were enclosed in the 18th and 19th centuries, the hayward was no longer required. In Downton, even after the 19th century enclosures, stray animals often wandered into the village from the New Forest until the mid 20th century and so the role remained useful. Downton's last hayward, George Futcher, held the position from 1897 until his death in 1940.

The document appointing George Futcher in 1897 lists his duties, thus providing an insight into the medieval past:

> the custom of the manor allows the Hayward to be paid his expenses on entering the hundred pound by whom the hundred pound is kept and custom is for him to take four pence per hoof for all cattle so held. Straid horses, cows, pigges and sheep and the cattle so strayed, must be cryed in two market towns immediately after their entry if the cattle so strayed should not be owned or claimed by the next court leet the jurie must present the cattle so straid otherwise the Lord can make no claim. After cattle have been straid and not owned it must remain twelve months and one day then sold to the best bidder to defray the expenses.[4]

The bishop of Winchester exercised meticulous control of the manor throughout the 13th century, generating much documentation which survives in the form of the Winchester Pipe Rolls. At Michaelmas a reeve collected rents and feudal dues and presented his record of the last year's obligations and discharges in the form of a *compotus* roll to the Bishop's bailiff. Downton had two reeves from 1208, one for the manor and one for the borough. The demands of the jobs necessitated that these village officials were literate. The Winchester Pipe Rolls were then compiled from the corrected *compotus* rolls at the bishop's palace at Wolvesey. They represent a fair copy of accounts presented by the reeve of each manor and borough to the bailiff. As such they run across two years, Michaelmas to Michaelmas. The first surviving roll dates from 1208-9, just after the foundation of the borough of Downton. They are challenging documents even for a scholar of the medieval period and few have been fully translated and published. However Dr. J.Z. Titow translated and published the 1208-9 roll for the manor of Downton in 1969.[5] It tells us, for example, that the bridge, though it is not specified which one, was repaired at a cost of 5 shillings plus the labour services of hauling gravel to the site. It also appears that the Lord Bishop stayed in Downton for a total of sixteen nights that year because the accounts allow for provender for his two horses during his stay. A great deal of produce from the manor went into the bishop's larder to allow for his lavish entertaining, both in Downton and presumably at Wolvesey (in Winchester) and also in London. In 1208-9 it included 4 piglets, 84 pigs and 273 hens. By contrast nine and a half pigs were provided to feed 55 men on the manor who undertook ploughing as labour services that year. Failure to perform these services, which included a variety of agricultural tasks meant a fine. For example:

> Edward Biliz was fined 18 pence for failure to sow one acre.

Manorial tenants also had to pay the bishop for permission to marry, take on land from a deceased tenant, graze animals on pasture, use the mill and collect wood. An entry in 1208-9 tells us that the following were collected:

> 6s 8d from William, son of Selida for having the land of Emma.
> And 10s from Walter for the marrying of his daughter

Misdemeanours were dealt with in the manorial court:

> Jordanus, son of Norman was fined 12 pence for an affray and
> Adam de Roxy had to pay 12 pence to recover his animals.

Presumably they had strayed and had been rounded up into the pound by the hayward.[6]

By contrast the management of the new borough was much less complicated than the management of the manor. This is vividly illustrated by the fact that the *burgus* or borough section in the Winchester Pipe Rolls usually comprised approximately half a dozen entries a year. By contrast the reeve's records for the manor covered four to six feet of closely written parchment, detailing feudal obligations and defaults. This shift towards a new money-based economy in Downton is illustrated by the presence of coins from the period which were found in the wall of an outhouse at Leicester House in The Borough, and a later 14th century King David of Scotland silver penny found in South Lane.

Following the establishment of the borough, the parish church was enlarged considerably, to cope with the growing population and to reflect the rising status of Downton. Two eastern bays were built onto the nave of the church, a central tower and transepts were added and the chancel was enlarged.[7] This was high quality work which may have attracted new tenants to the borough.[8] The church services were, as everywhere in the country at that time, Catholic and by 1350 the simple Saxon church of Downton had been completely replaced by a magnificent newly decorated church, typical of the faith at that time. It probably contained fine carvings in stone and wood, depicting saints and the Virgin Mary. The walls were covered in richly coloured paintings and together with the stained glass windows they brought to life the stories of the Bible and were an education for a largely illiterate population. As services were conducted exclusively in Latin and the Bible was not yet translated into English, this was a method by which important religious lessons were taught to the congregation. The elaborate workmanship was also a symbol of the power of the medieval church to humble villagers.

Bishop Peter des Roches was an influential man of his time; he came from Poitou in Northern France and was appointed bishop of Winchester in 1205. He was a loyal servant of King John throughout his reign, even supporting John during the crisis with his nobles which led to the signing of Magna Carta in 1215. He was later guardian to the young Henry III. Des Roches' biographer, Nicholas Vincent describes him as a 'courtier of genius'.[9] It seems likely that such a skilful administrator who cultivated his own court of influential Norman officials received royal visits, and King John is thought to have visited the bishop in Downton at least four times, in 1206, 1207, 1209 and 1215.[10] The old palace adjacent to the present site of the

A bust in the alcove of the White Horse Inn.

Moot was rebuilt or refurbished at this time to accommodate royal visitors. It was renamed King John's Palace. Two hundred years later the building was referred to as the Old Court because a new manorial centre or New Court replaced it on a site west of the Avon. Local tradition suggests that some of the masonry from Old Court was re-used in buildings in The Borough, which seems probable, and that the two busts inserted into alcoves in the front wall of the White Horse Inn are in fact busts of King John and Queen Isabel although some experts believe they are 18th century replicas.[11] Elsewhere it has been suggested that they represent John the Baptist and Mary and may have been rescued from a church in the Reformation.[12]

Investment in the manor of Downton continued after the establishment of the new borough. Throughout the 13th century the manor of Downton was managed intensively with an eye to greater profits for the lord bishop. There was an attempt to conserve and improve soil fertility by manuring. Tenants holding one virgate (about 30 acres) had to carry between thirteen and twenty-five loads of dung to manure the Lord's demesne land each year. Arable crops were mainly wheat, oats and barley and tenants were obliged to carry their master's harvest to market in their own carts. Wool was a key product and the lord bishop's flocks on all his manors were managed as a whole by a supervisor of flocks and tended locally by paid shepherds, aided by labour services of tenants. This included driving sheep and making hurdles. However sheep deaths from disease were very high with up to 50% being lost in a bad year from unknown maladies. Some of

The Borough flooded in 1915 as it had done regularly for centuries (Margaret Smith).

the lord bishop's tenants also had flocks of their own and they could pasture them with the demesne flocks for a payment in kind of one in ten sheep.

Some of the profits of the manor were spent in 1235 on improving the great hall, most probably in the bishop's palace in Downton and in 1251 a new barn was erected. One interesting feature of the manorial system in Downton was that virgaters had to attend the annual 'scotale', for which they had each to pay two and a half pence. This was a customary ale-drinking session which lasted about two days.[13] Another feature of this annual occasion was the requirement that wives had to attend as well.

Yet in spite of the Bishop's investment in both his Downton manor and the borough of Downton, with its early growth and its new town status, the settlement failed to develop further and it remained in a sense a village. There was a steady increase in the number of tenants of the borough from 19 in 1205 to 120 in the 1230s but growth of the borough soon faltered and Downton never urbanised. This failure to grow into a sizeable market town was probably due to several factors. One was the regular flooding from the River Avon, calling into question the original siting of The Borough. Another factor was the proximity of Downton to the fast developing city of Salisbury.

The Black Death in Downton

Throughout the 13th and early 14th century until the time of the Black Death there was an extension of arable cultivation beyond the flood plain to the gently sloping valley sides, formerly used for pasture, and there may well have been settlements on higher ground for the first time. At least two areas of wooded land clearance were undertaken, at "Timberhill" and at "Cowyk". At the same time there was a decline in demesne arable acreage in Downton from 838 acres in 1208 to 300 acres by 1347. Between 1315 and 1322 a period of unusually bad weather in England led to famine which accelerated the move away from direct cultivation of the demesne land by lords towards leasing. On the Winchester estates as a whole the death rate rose by about 10% as shown by the rise in death duties recorded. However an even greater catastrophe was to come in 1349.

Downton was badly affected by the Black Death. In 1348 the disease struck England, being first reported in the Dorset town of Melcombe Regis. The effects were devastating. Its symptoms are not described locally but were vividly described by Giovanni Boccaccio in the Decameron:

> The first signs of the plague were lumps in the groin or armpits.

The Borough of Downton

After this, livid black spots appeared on the arms and thighs and other parts of the body. Few recovered. Almost all died within three days, usually without any fever.

Nationally it killed approximately 1.5 million out of a population of 4 million. There was no antidote and no cure. The rapid spread of the disease meant that it would have been almost impossible for people to cope with its immediate effects and undoubtedly bodies would have lain unburied in cottages and in the open.

The effects of the the Black Death in Downton have never been fully studied except as a part of the Winchester estate. However the Winchester Pipe Roll for the year 1349-50 reveals a tragic story. When the disease hit the area in 1349 a new section appeared in the Pipe Rolls, 'defectus per pestilenciam' which translates as defaults due to the plague. Previously scribes had meticulously maintained the same format for recording by hand on vellum rolls every penny received and spent and they had always used the same sections and headings. In the first full year of the plague, there were so many defaults of rent that this special new section was created. In 1349, 75 tenants were listed as having defaulted because of death from the plague, out of a total of 150 tenants. They included John of Downton, John Dygge, William Hull, Thomas Papel, John White and John Foucher. The men listed were heads of households; their wives, children and elderly relatives were not listed but it is likely that a far greater proportion of the very old and the very young died than the relatively robust heads of household. The death rate in Downton was estimated as high as 66% of the total population by Professor Elizabeth Leggett, who calculated the immediate effect of the Black Death by studying the heriots received by the Bishop of Winchester that year, heriots being a form of death duty owed by tenants. This figure was also agreed in another study of the Winchester estates by Titow.[14] It may have been even higher than the list of defaults suggests because tenants who replaced plague victims frequently died themselves soon after. So it seems that at least as many and probably more died in Downton in the first wave of the plague than the death rate nationally. Why this happened is not clear but it could be explained by one of the factors which led to the development of Downton in Saxon times, its location at the crossing point of the river. This had the effect of channelling travellers carrying the deadly virus through the heart of the village.

Defaults and acquittances (temporary excusal) due to the plague in 1349 amounted to £25 3s. 1d. in lost rent. To give some idea of the relative significance of this figure, it should be noted that the total of rents collected that year amounted to £55 2s. 6d. and defaults for

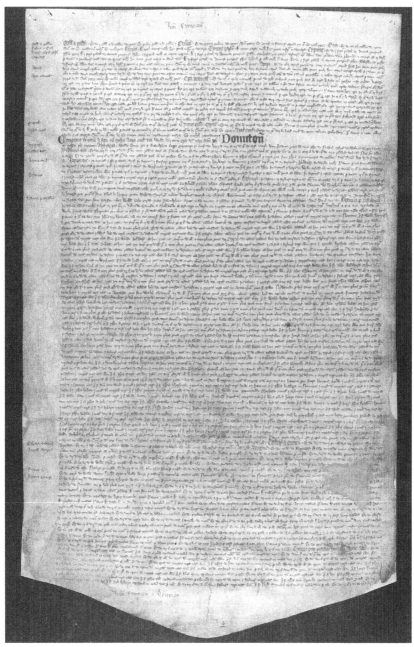

The section of the 1348-9 Winchester Pipe Roll which lists defaults of rent
due to the plague in Downton (HRO 11M59/B1/102).

reasons other than plague amounted to a mere £2 16s. In the previous
year the total default amounted to £6 7s. 1d. The Pipe Rolls used for

the mundane purpose of accounting for the income and expenditure of the manor and the borough reveal a sad story of pestilence, death and human loss on a massive scale.[15]

Despite this, it was not difficult for the lord bishop to find new manorial tenants as this was a rich and fertile valley. Downton was clearly a desirable holding and in the few years after the first occurrence of the plague, the lord bishop actually increased his profits because his receipt of death duties and entry fines increased. It was the marginal, upland settlements which shrank most rapidly. In Downton it is debatable whether fields were left unploughed and the harvests uncollected but over time arable acreage shrank and food shortages particularly of bread led to inflated prices, malnutrition and death from causes other than the pestilence. In England as a whole there was an increase of pasture animals, particularly sheep because they required less intensive labour and with the rapid fall in population more holdings became vacant and tenants fortunate enough to survive the disease could acquire more land. With fewer numbers they were able to negotiate more favourable terms of tenancy with landlords desperate to find any tenant at all. In Downton labour services were frequently not performed and the result was, in the words of Mark Page, who translated and compared the Winchester Pipe Rolls of 1301-2 with those of 1409-10, 'the balance of power shifted from landlord to tenant.'[16]

Nearly thirty years after the Black Death there was a recovery in Downton's population. By 1377, the bishop had 150 tenants again, but it is probable that many were incomers to the manor who were able to negotiate better terms. The bishop's rental income from Downton increased with proportionately more rent than feudal dues. Peasants in Downton and all over the country were being freed from serfdom because they simply paid a money rent rather than labour services as in the old feudal system.[17] Feudal law had dictated that peasants could only leave their village with the lord of the manor's permission. After 1349 and with a subsequent labour shortage caused by the Black Death many lords actively persuaded peasants to leave neighbouring villages to become their tenants or work for them for a wage.

In 1351 the government introduced the Statute of Labourers to control peasants roaming around the countryside looking for better pay. It stated that no peasants could be paid more than the level of wages paid in 1346 and reaffirmed that peasants could not leave their villages without their lord's permission. The ruling caused considerable resentment and was largely ignored. Although the subsequent unrest centred mainly in the South East and London, it is likely that village people who had survived the plague emerged with a better quality of life once the unrest died down.

There were several subsequent outbreaks of plague, and the 1409-10 Pipe Roll reveals that in Downton that year there were 11 defaults of rent 'per pestilenciam'.[18] The plague victims included Robert Judde, John Clement and Robert Mody, possibly an ancestor of the present day Moody family of Downton. One interesting feature of the later rolls is the adoption of many more recognisable surnames, where previously several tenants were referred to by christian names only. So in 1409-10 we can see that the reeve of Downton manor was Ralph Elyot and the reeve of Downton borough was Ralph Fotere.

Winchester College

There was a further important development in the history of Downton before the end of the 14th century. In 1380 William Wykeham, then bishop of Winchester, wanted to endow a college for the maintenance of 70 poor scholars in Winchester. Wykeham, born in Wickham, Hampshire, was a self-made man who had risen to high office and he was keen to ensure the education of future clergy for the church. Initially he paid from his own pocket for a schoolmaster to educate 70 poor scholars. To achieve more he decided that tithes collected from Downton would provide the extra funds needed for his new venture.

At the time the tithes of Downton, which were not inconsiderable, were collected and retained by the rector, an appointee of the bishop.[19] Wykeham obtained the permission of King Richard II to appropriate the tithes from Downton for the maintenance of his scholars. In effect he took the rector of Downton's income and in its place set aside an endowment to maintain a vicar in Downton, rather than a rector. The new arrangement allowed the vicar to receive a smaller tithe which included swans and peacocks for the table.[20]

Downton's last rector was Nicholas de Alresford and in 1385 he became the first vicar of Downton. The parsonage had previously been the dwelling for the village chaplain, appointed by the rector to perform his pastoral duties. It was improved for the vicar by the bishop and given more land, running up to Barford Lane. Formerly known as Parsonage Manor, it is now the Manor House. It is one of the oldest continuously inhabited houses in England, and still contains sections dating from the 14th century. The name 'parsonage' still survives in Parsonage Farm in Barford Lane.

William Wykeham's vision and successful petition to the king led to the foundation of the famous public school Winchester College.

Parsonage Manor and the parish church of St. Laurence, taken in the 1950s (Margaret Smith).

Building began in 1387 and it has functioned continuously from 1394 until the present day. In 1413 the vicar of Downton, Thomas Stratton, complained that his endowment was insufficient and took action against Winchester College but the judgement favoured the new school. However Downton benefited in a small way because the College was tasked to educate a number of Downton boys. Winchester College archives reveal that 22 boys from Downton were educated between 1394 and 1633.[21]

By the mid 14th century the income from the manor of Downton had shrunk and in 1551 the manor was leased in its entirety to William Herbert. Leasing was less risky as it provided a steady income for the Lord Bishop. As the lessee Herbert paid a fixed rent to Winchester and had the right to exercise manorial control including some legal jurisdiction. In 1534 William Herbert had married Anne Parr, sister of Catherine Parr, the fifth wife of King Henry VIII. As a valued and loyal courtier, he was later appointed as one of the guardians to the young Edward VI when he succeeded to the throne in 1547. He was created earl of Pembroke in the same year that he acquired the lease on Downton. He already owned the old abbey buildings at Wilton and had begun transforming them into a home fit for a man of his status, Wilton House.

The association of Downton with the Herberts, a family who served royalty through several generations, continued for the next hundred years. Downton was entering a new age, one in which its fortunes were dominated by a number of influential families.

5

Tudors & Stuarts

Downton initially saw no obvious changes with the establishment of the Tudor dynasty by Henry VII in 1485. It was the Reformation of the later Tudors which affected the people of Downton more profoundly, as it did everyone in England. When Henry VIII was refused a papal annulment of his marriage to Queen Catherine of Aragon there was a formal break from Rome although doctrinally Henry VIII and his realm remained Catholic for the time being. In 1534 parliament, skilfully managed by Thomas Cromwell, obliged Henry VIII by passing an Act of Supremacy which made the monarch supreme head of the church in England.

Even at this point changes were not immediately obvious in the parishes of England either in church decor, religious teachings or services. The first effect of religious policy would have become apparent in the Downton area a little later. In 1536 Henry VIII's Lord Chancellor Thomas Cromwell investigated monastic life in England leading to the widespread dissolution of monasteries, abbeys and nunneries. Many had retained an important social function in medieval times, providing physical as well as spiritual care. A decree issued by Winchester in 1327 had stated that apart from the observance of daily masses, the monks of St Michael's Priory, Breamore should give alms to the poor and administer to the sick. But Breamore Priory and Wilton Abbey, both situated within ten miles of Downton, were closed down by Cromwell's commissioners and their buildings and land were awarded to favourites of the King. Wilton Abbey was sold to Sir William Herbert, a rising star in royal circles, who was also to take over the lease of Downton manor in 1551. Breamore Priory eventually found its way into the hands of the Dodington family. At

Sir Walter Raleigh: Portrait discovered in the Manor House (National Portrait Gallery).

Wilton the abbey buildings became the foundation for a magnificent stately home. Breamore Priory, sited between the modern A338 and the River Avon, fell into ruin and Sir William Dodington later built Breamore House on higher ground to the west of the current road. There is no record of how these developments were received locally.

Downton witnessed further religious changes in the reign of Henry VIII's son Edward VI, when a medieval wall painting below the west window of St. Laurence church was painted over during the Reformation. The painting possibly depicted the biblical tale of the flight into Egypt.[1] In the spirit of the age, the richness of church decoration, which represented the wealth of the Church in Rome, was considered unsuitable and plain walls were favoured. A thorough religious reformation was taking place, masterminded by Thomas Cranmer, Archbishop of Canterbury and Edward Seymour, Duke of Somerset, the young King Edward VI's Lord Protector. The Special Injunction banned most traditional Catholic customs, practices and ceremonies. Religious statues of saints were sold or smashed, stained glass windows were replaced with plain ones and there must have been a good trade in lime wash as wall paintings inside most parish churches were painted over. This was equally true of highly decorated windows and in St. Laurence Church there remains no medieval glass except that placed in the window in the north aisle. The parish church also lost its medieval rood, a crucifix set on a beam, which would have rested on the corbels of the fourth pillars from the west end on either side of the nave. The corbels can still be seen, the rood and rood screen were considered too idolatrous.

Downton remained a relatively small borough in the 16th century. Its fate lay in the hands of a few great men, the movers and shakers of the English Reformation. This was not only due to the injunctions of Edward VI but also because it was still one of the most important manors in the Bishop of Winchester's estate. Cardinal Wolsey, blamed for his failure to resolve the issue of Henry VIII's divorce from Catherine of Aragon, had been Bishop of Winchester from 1529 to 1531 as well as Lord Chancellor of England. He was succeeded as Bishop of Winchester by Stephen Gardiner, a powerful diplomat and courtier of Henry VIII. Gardiner had fallen out with Henry's son Edward VI as he objected to the extreme religious changes brought about in Edward's name, stating that such measures should not have been undertaken in the King's minority. Edward succeeded to the throne aged nine and died at fifteen years old. Gardiner was imprisoned in the Tower of London. His successor as Bishop of Winchester was John Ponet, an influential Protestant theologian with a colourful private life. It seems Ponet married while still a Catholic priest at a time when the church enforced celibacy and his marriage was later annulled on the grounds that his wife was married to a Nottinghamshire butcher. Ponet was an ally of Edward VI's protector, Edward Seymour Duke of Somerset and when Seymour fell from power in 1549 so did Ponet. It was at this point that Ponet was compelled to surrender many of his lands including Downton to Edward VI who in turn leased the lordship of Downton in 1551 to Sir William Herbert.

Sir William Herbert was at this time a member of the Privy Council. He occupied a privileged position in royal circles and was rewarded with an earldom by the young king, Edward VI. As 1st earl of Pembroke he entertained Edward VI at Wilton House in 1552. A staunch Protestant, we can safely assume he would have carried out Edward VI's religious injunctions. The congregation of Downton church would have seen these changes enforced.

In 1553 the lease of Downton was cancelled by royal warrant by Queen Mary I who succeeded her brother Edward VI. She was determined to restore Catholicism. Gardiner was reinstated as bishop of Winchester and it was a sign of Queen Mary's esteem for him that he was asked to conduct her marriage to Phillip II of Spain in Winchester Cathedral. In 1558 Mary granted John White, Gardiner's successor as bishop of Winchester, the episcopal lands including Downton manor so they again returned to the control of a churchman. In Downton the election of John Stone in 1558 as one of its two MPs is also a clear indication of the return of Catholic supremacy. John Stone was a servant of the bishop of Winchester and a zealous Catholic. Originally a Salisbury man he studied law at Oxford and on one occasion was imprisoned for insolence to his principal. He was also banished for further insolence to the judge hearing his case. Incensed by the Protestant Reformation of Edward VI, his fiery temper and religious extremism frequently got him into trouble. According to Foxe he once came straight from the burning of a protestant martyr to a banquet, boasting that he had dispatched one as he would do the rest.[2]

With the accession to the throne of Elizabeth I towards the end of 1558 the lease of Downton manor was renewed. The practice of leasing the manor or portions of it to tenants had become commonplace at this time probably due to a period of falling agricultural income. Downton's MP John Stone found himself once more on the wrong side of the law and spoke angrily against Queen Elizabeth I in parliament. His staunch Catholicism was eventually to cost him his life.

Elizabeth I and the Raleighs

The influence of Elizabeth I was clearly felt in Downton. Her religious settlement affirmed the status of the Anglican church as the state religion while still allowing Catholics to worship in private. This decree was accepted by all but fifteen priests in Wiltshire. In 1581 Parsonage Manor and the glebe or church land were leased to the Queen for £4 4s. 5d. per annum. The letter from Elizabeth asking for the lease no longer exists but a draft reply from Winchester College does survive. It shows that the College tried to excuse itself from this request for reasons unknown but Sir Christopher Hatton,[3] the earl of Leicester and Sir Francis Walsingham all urged the College to agree which they did reluctantly.[4] Parsonage Manor, the vicar's residence given as part of his benefice, was already an old property by this time, the oldest part of the house dating from the 14th century.

There is no evidence that Elizabeth I visited Downton. Her sole reason for acquiring the lease, as was the case with numerous properties, was to pass it on as a reward to a faithful servant, in this case Thomas Wilkes of London, the clerk to the Privy Council. It may have been his influence which led to the appointment of his cousin, William Wilkes, as vicar of Downton in 1587.

Thomas Wilkes in turn assigned the lease to the Raleigh family. The Raleighs remained in residence for a hundred years and were one of Downton's most important families during this period. By the early 1600s the lease of Parsonage Manor had passed to Sir Carew Raleigh, elder brother of the famous Sir Walter Raleigh, the explorer and favourite of Queen Elizabeth I. Sir Carew's second son, Gilbert, was born in Downton and it seems likely that Sir Walter Raleigh visited Downton on several occasions as he was godfather to Gilbert. An original portrait of Sir Walter Raleigh was discovered in the oak panelling in the parlour of Parsonage Manor in the mid 18th century. Sir Walter cuts a dashing figure with curly brown hair, a white satin doublet and two pearl earrings in his ear. The diarist John Aubrey visited the house in about 1669 and he recorded having seen it there. The painting was sold to the National Portrait Gallery for one hundred guineas in 1857 and it was the first picture ever purchased by the Gallery, rather than being donated.[5]

A story recounted locally is that the Queen intended to visit the

The Manor House (Margaret Smith).

Raleighs at Downton on her way to the newly built Breamore House. This supposedly caused a panic because Parsonage Manor was not considered grand enough to receive her. The legend recites that Sir Walter sailed a ship up the Avon to Downton so that its timbers could be used to refurbish the house. There are indeed ship's timbers in the house and it is well known that Elizabeth I travelled around her kingdom in search of hospitality, but there is no evidence that she actually visited Breamore or indeed Downton. The story is highly implausible for two reasons. One is that the River Avon was barely navigable at that time and certainly not for a large ship. Secondly if it were possible, it would have taken weeks to drag a ship up river, hardly a sensible decision if timber was needed in a hurry and when a plentiful supply of timber was available in the New Forest. It was not unusual for timbers to be re-used but in this case they were more likely to have come from the shipyard at Beaulieu.

There is however evidence that Queen Elizabeth I visited Wilton House, which in the later years of her reign was a centre of culture under the patronage of the second Countess of Pembroke Mary Sidney, sister of Sir Philip Sidney. She may have passed through Downton to visit the Raleighs while in the area but we will probably never know.

Meanwhile the daily toil continued for Downton's lesser inhabitants. There were several serious floods in Downton in the 1600s, at least one of which generated an appeal by the curate of Downton to the Wiltshire Quarter Sessions. It appeared that residents were expected to carry travellers through the flood waters or face arrest for failing to do so when asked. When the road between the Mill Bridge and Catherine Bridge flooded in 1631 the curate asked the court that old people might be excused their obligations of carrying travellers. John Eastman is mentioned as one of the Downton residents who contacted the curate to ask for assistance in this matter.[6]

The Raleigh family continued to live in Downton until 1698 on the death of Sir Charles Raleigh, a descendant of Carew. Raleighs periodically served as MPs for Downton and the family was clearly very wealthy, as evidenced by Sir Charles Raleigh's will. His total assets were £4,687 at his death.

The occupancy by the Raleigh family of Parsonage Manor House, discreetly tucked away behind the church, spans the reigns of the last Tudor monarch Elizabeth I through to the tumultuous years of the Stuart kings and the Protectorate of Oliver Cromwell. These momentous national events affirmed the supremacy of parliament over the monarchy and helped to secure the nation's democratic rights. The closest Downton came to any serious action during the period of the English Civil War was an uprising in Salisbury against Cromwell.[7]

The city supported King Charles I and its royalist leader was Colonel John Penruddock who was captured by Cromwell's forces, taken to Exeter and executed in 1655.[8] Penruddock's daughter Joanne was married to Maurice Bockland of Standlynch Manor. Joanne rebuilt the Standlynch chapel which was originally established in 1147. A later chapel on the site, now disused but owned by Michael Wade who also owns Trafalgar House, contains a memorial to Joanne, describing her 'deep sense of zeal and pious virtue'.[9] It is possible that the stone cross, which stands outside the White Horse in Downton, was damaged during the Civil War by Oliver Cromwell's forces. This cross, which had previously surmounted the monument, was found in the garden of Fairfield House during restoration work in 1953 and it has been suggested that it had lain there since it was torn off by Puritan parliamentarians who hated any symbol of Catholicism.

In 1642 in the Wiltshire Quarter Sessions the court agreed to continue paying relief for Samuel Lynch of Downton, who is one of only two Downton men recorded to have fought in the civil war between crown and parliament. It was customary for wounded soldiers to be awarded help. No details of Lynch's regiment or his injuries are given, but he can be assumed to have been fighting for the king because the award was made by John Penruddock and Edward Hyde, 1st earl of Clarendon, both royalists, who sat in judgement. [10]

A second Downton man to have fought as a soldier in the civil war was Thomas Champion. He fought for parliament for five years

The Borough Cross shortly after restoration after the Second World War (Margaret Smith).

in Colonel Hewson's regiment in Kent, where he was shot in both legs. His debilitating injuries were certified by his commanding officer, Colonel Axtell, who wrote to the court to say that Champion had a wife and three children and 'nothing to maintain them'. He was awarded a pension of £4 per annum in October 1649, during the Protectorate.[11] During the period when the country was ruled by Oliver Cromwell and after his death in 1658 briefly by his son, that is 1648 to 1660, only parliamentarian soldiers were awarded pensions.

The civil war brought not only political animosities to the fore but also religious ones, because of the predominantly Puritan nature of the forces of parliament who opposed the suspiciously Catholic leanings of King Charles I. In the year of Charles's execution, 1649, the court was informed by Revd. Samuel Cox, vicar of Downton, that some popish recusants were living in the village with their cousin Mr. Stockman. Recusants were Catholics who did not attend Anglican services. Cox stated that he had tried to 'turn them from popery and so far failed'. He advised Stockman not to keep them in his house any longer but added, 'though their case be to be pitied (*sic*) for their temporal as well as their spiritual well-being'.[12] Cox seemed to have been a man who regretted the bitterness of religious arguments and their human and spiritual cost.

On the subject of religious loyalties an examination of the Bockland family of Standlynch is worthy of a digression. Walter Bockland served as an MP for Downton between 1661 and 1670. He inherited Standlynch House which had been originally purchased by his grandfather. A Catholic recusant, he fought on the Royalist side in the Civil War but was persuaded after the war to swear that he was an Anglican to avoid forfeiting his estate. Fortunately for him he had been baptised an Anglican, yet he almost certainly retained his Catholic sympathies until he died, and he may have been involved in Penruddock's uprising, as Penruddock was his father-in law.

His son Maurice Bockland was a long serving Downton MP (1678-95) and owing to his family background he had to convince parliament of his loyalty to the Anglican faith and to the state at a time when England remained deeply opposed to Catholicism. Catholics were forbidden from holding public office under the Test Act. In his defence his colleague and fellow Downton MP, Sir Joseph Ashe, publicly stated that, 'he hath shown his opinion to be against popery'. Bockland cannily voted in favour of tougher measures against recusants, even though his parents were counted among them, but he remained ambivalent about his faith during the crisis brought about by the accession of the Catholic James II to the throne in 1685. Ostensibly a Whig whose adherents were opposed to James II, he once stated that as an elected representative he must serve his king. He was equally evasive on the proposal to repeal the Test Act. He may well have kept out of trouble due to his association with Sir Joseph Ashe, who similarly needed Bockland on-side for his proposed water meadow scheme in Downton, which required the destruction of one of Bockland's mills at Standlynch.

The opinions of most of the inhabitants of Downton at this time can only be guessed at. They probably continued their lives with little awareness of national events. Almost the only way of receiving news of the outside world was through the town crier, who rang his bell through the streets making proclamations.[13]

By the late 17th century Downton remained a fairly busy small town with a mixed population of farmers, craftsmen, traders, shopkeepers, innkeepers as well as wealthy landowners. But the zenith of the Wiltshire woollen trade passed in the mid-16th century after which the population and relative wealth of the area declined. Despite the growth and influence of parliament in national life, only a few Downton men were entitled to vote for their representatives in the House of Commons. The ambitions of the former bishop of Winchester Peter des Roches to create a thriving market town had barely been realised. Downton had failed to develop fully as a town of independent burgesses, and most burgage properties which had the right to vote attached to them were owned by a handful of important landowners, who in turn controlled the election of MPs. Social mobility was more advanced in neighbouring Salisbury.

There were other wealthy families who left their mark on Downton. One was the Stockman family who leased Barford Park from Winchester at this time. William Stockman was born there in 1540 and in 1603 he became one of Downton's MPs. He died in 1626 and in his will he gave:

> Chadwell Farm in White Parish and directed that the rents should be distributed yearly among ... poor persons ... within the said Parish (Downton).[14]

The bequest consisted of 60 acres and six cottages. The charity survives today as the Stockman and Woodlands Trust (so named in 1970 because John Woodlands had donated £1,000 to the trustees in his will in 1881) and it continues to make small donations to people in need in Downton and locally.

In 1662 the lease of Downton Manor passed from Philip Herbert, earl of Pembroke to Sir Joseph Ashe, a very wealthy London businessman based in Twickenham. The Ashe family had made their money as cloth

New Court Farm House.

manufacturers. Sir Joseph was already the owner of New Court Farm, which he purchased in 1649. He represented Downton in parliament from 1678 to 1685 but was a fairly inactive member, at one point being forced to defend himself against an accusation of low attendance in the House. Like his colleague Maurice Bockland, he may well have had Catholic and Royalist sympathies but was not involved in fighting in the Civil War, instead preferring to remain abroad. There is a suspicion that he may have passed funds to the Royalists through his association with the Shaws, a Royalist family connected to his niece by marriage. He was clever enough to cover any traces and apart from his defence of Maurice Bockland's Anglican sympathies, appears to have acted tactfully in order to maintain his power and influence nationally and in Downton.

Ashe was responsible for a notable Downton landmark. He was a man in tune with the latest agricultural developments and he set to work establishing water meadows in what is now Catherine Meadow.[15] In the 1680s he rebuilt the farm house at New Court on a lavish scale and added two aisled barns. The house survives, the barns do not, one was burnt down shortly after the Second World War and the other, although a listed building which villagers remember as a magnificent timber framed barn, was demolished in the 1970s. Clear traces of the water meadows can still be seen but there has been no policy towards their conservation.[16] At this time work also began on making the Avon navigable as far as Salisbury. The project was completed in 1687 but the navigation was little used and by the 1750s it had fallen into disuse.[17]

Sir Joseph Ashe also helped to establish the Downton Grammar Free School although his bequest to the school in his will of £100 seems small in comparison to the £7,000 he left to each of his unmarried daughters by the same testament. He died in 1686 and is buried in Twickenham, where he has a fine memorial in the parish church. An interest in agricultural innovation continued in the family when his grandson, Charles, 2nd viscount Townshend, nicknamed *Turnip Townshend,* developed a system of four course rotation of crops on his Norfolk estate at Raynham Park.[18]

Two more great houses were built in Downton in this period. Moot House was constructed in about 1690, probably by the Cole family. In 1784 it was inherited by Charles Shuckburgh and it was passed down the family until it it was sold to Elias Pitt Squarey, a gentleman farmer, in 1864.[19] The other was Barford House which was built by Charles Duncombe at about the same time. Moot House survives but all that is left of Barford House is a partial avenue of trees which now leads to Barford Park Farm.

In the late 17th century the south west of England was at the centre of the Monmouth Rebellion and before his capture near Ringwood the duke of Monmouth's escape route may have passed through Downton. In May 1685 the duke of Monmouth claimed the

The Great Barn at New Court (Historic England BB71/00470).

throne of England. He landed at Lyme Regis with three small ships and about 300 men, later rising to about 1,500.[20] He quickly gathered local supporters of Protestant and Non-Conformist persuasion, many committed to deposing the Catholic King James II. Men also supported the rebellion for economic as well as political reasons as there was increasing rural poverty in the area. The rebellion was centred in Dorset, Somerset and Devon and there was a skirmish in Trowbridge. The Wiltshire Militia was called to action to defend the Crown, although the government did not specifically see Wiltshire as a county which harboured Monmouth supporters. They found it necessary to ask the constables of Dorset, Somerset and Devon to report men absent from home but not in Wiltshire.[21]

Monmouth fled after the Battle of Sedgemoor which took place in 1685 in Somerset, intending to reach Poole Harbour to escape by sea. His escape route was via Salisbury and almost certainly went though Downton as he was captured near Ringwood, sleeping in a ditch near Horton. The government sought terrible retribution against his supporters in the Bloody Assizes conducted by Judge Jeffreys. The Assizes passed through Winchester, Salisbury and Dorchester, though no record has been found of any Downton men being involved.

In 1686 Sir Joseph Ashe of New Court died. His son Sir James Ashe succeeded him. Like his father he served Downton as one of its two MPs, between 1701 and 1705, but was apparently a pale shadow of his father in terms of energy and enterprise. In 1741 he sold the lease of Downton Manor to Anthony Duncombe, whose family was soon to be linked with the Bouveries, now the earls of Radnor, by marriage. The story of their battle for control of elections in Downton is told in the next chapter.

6

Influential Families

In the 18th century Downton was controlled by two families of wealth and power. Their rivalry creates a fascinating story of the struggle for political influence and democratic rights. Not long after, in 1832 the borough of Downton was disenfranchised and lost its status of having two members of parliament. What follows is an explanation of how and why this happened.

The emergence of democracy in Britain is a fascinating narrative. Events from the outbreak of the English Civil War in 1642 to the Glorious Revolution of 1689 resulted in the supremacy of parliament over the crown. Yet parliament's House of Commons did not represent all citizens until modern times. Until the early 19th century the right to vote for members of parliament was inconsistent and arbitrary and there were many anomalies and injustices regarding enfranchisement in Downton and elsewhere in the country.

As a borough Downton had the right to send two MPs to the House of Commons. It was a privilege enjoyed by approximately six Wiltshire towns of a similar size.[1] In spite of its status as a borough few were entitled to vote because Downton was a *pocket borough*. Its two MPs were in the pocket of landlords who strongly influenced the small electorate to vote for their chosen candidates. In the late 18th century this led to a series of famously disputed elections between the two wealthy landowning families, the Duncombes and the Bouveries.

The Duncombe family's association with Downton dates back to 1690 when Sir Charles Duncombe built Barford House. He represented Downton in parliament from 1695 until 1698 and again from 1702 until his death in 1711. Before his political career Duncombe had made a vast fortune as a goldsmith and banker, at one

The Duncombe Memorial in St. Laurence Church.

time to King Charles II, and was Lord Mayor of London in 1708. He had been accused of corruption and was briefly imprisoned in the Tower before being acquitted. Among his many enemies the famous writer Daniel Defoe described him thus:

> Duncombe, the modern Judas of the age,
> Has often tried in vain to mount the stage:
> Profuse in gifts and bribes to God and man,
> To ride the City horse and wear the chain[2]

He is buried in the south transept of St Laurence church where he has a fine memorial. He remained unmarried throughout his life although there were suggestions of many mistresses. He died intestate leaving no children and on his death his estate was divided between two nephews who were cousins to each other and a niece. The younger nephew Anthony Duncombe inherited the Downton and Barford properties. He became Lord Feversham in 1747.

Anthony Lord Feversham followed his uncle into parliament, representing Downton between 1734 and 1747. By contrast with his uncle his parliamentary career was unspectacular. He was married for forty years to Margaret Verney but all their children predeceased her including the son and heir George at the age of 19. The first Lady Feversham, Margaret, is commemorated in a beautifully sculptured memorial by Scheemakers in St.Laurence Church. This describes her as:

> Remarkable for the beauty of her person and the sweetness of her manner.
> Bereaved of all her children (the last of which and the sole remaining hope of the family was just upon the verge of manhood). She bare (*sic*) it with the most perfect resignation to the will of God.

Lord Feversham married his second wife Frances Bathurst of Clarendon Park. She died giving birth to their daughter Frances. His third wife was Anne Hales of Kent who bore him a daughter also called Anne.

The Duncombes measured their power and position not just in real estate but in political influence. Anthony Lord Feversham owned the burgage or borough properties which his uncle had purchased in

Lady Feversham's memorial in St. Laurence Church.

order to secure a safe parliamentary seat. In 1741 he bought the lease of the manor of Downton which gave him the right to appoint the returning officer, one of whose roles was to count the votes cast at a parliamentary election. Feversham added to this estate by purchasing nine additional burgage properties from John Elliot and in 1742 to further secure the constituency he purchased the lease of the New Court estate from Sir Joseph Ashe. The burgage holding gave him control of the election as the number of voters, according the History of Parliament website is estimated to have been only about 100.[3] The tenants of these properties were entitled to vote and would have been persuaded by their positions as tenants to their landlord to choose the Duncombe candidate as there was no secret ballot.[4]

When he died in 1763 Lord Feversham thus left two daughters, one by the deceased Frances and a second by Anne but no male heir. His will created a feud. He left his Yorkshire Helmsley estate to the elder nephew's son, Thomas, as well as the Barford estate and three-quarters of the burgage properties in Downton, those which he inherited from his uncle. His three year old daughter Anne was left the remaining Downton properties and the manor of Downton with its right to choose the returning officer. There was a provision in the will which required that on the sale of Anne's Downton properties Thomas would have first right to acquire them. It was this clause which was to be successfully challenged in the Court of Chancery by the Bouverie family. Feversham's widow Anne was still a relatively young woman when, two years later she married William Bouverie, viscount Folkestone who would that year succeed his father as earl of Radnor. The Bouveries were large landowners with a family seat at Longford Castle.[5]

Thomas Duncombe of the Yorkshire branch of the family had a daughter, also called Anne, who married Robert Shafto. Bobby Shafto, as he was nicknamed, played a part in the history of Downton too. He is immortalised in a traditional song or nursery rhyme which may have been written about him or used by him later as an election promotion. One theory is that the song refers to his dashing good looks and the fact that he broke the heart of Bridget Belasyse of Brancepeth Castle when he married into the Duncombe family. He had previously been engaged to Bridget. She died two weeks after hearing the news of his marriage.

When Shafto married Anne of the Yorkshire Duncombes and first stood for parliament in Downton this created a conflict of influence because a large number of burgage properties belonged to his wife's family and another proportion were held by Lord Feversham's executors on behalf of Anne, the wife of William Bouverie earl of

Radnor. From 1774 the divisive political influence of the two families led to a series of famously contested elections. The dispute heated up when the Yorkshire Thomas Duncombe died in 1780 and his interest in the Downton seat passed to Shafto. It centred on the appointment of the legal returning officer, whose duty was the counting of hands on election day and determining the final election result. The Duncombes claimed the appointee should be their bailiff and the Radnors claimed the position for their steward. The loyalties of the rival returning officers, it was later claimed in court, affected the count so that in the two parliamentary elections of 1784 two different results were given.[6]

The long running argument was reported in Luders, *Reports of Proceedings in Committees of the House of Commons Upon Contraverted Elections,* in 1785 with Shafto alleging:

> that Henry Harrison, Esq: was the legal returning officer, that his return was the legal one ... that John Dagge, gent. had, without right taken it upon himself to act as returning officer and had rejected many legal votes for the petitioners.

While Luders reports in contrast:

> The petition of Bouverie and Scott set forth that the legal returning officer of the borough is the bailiff or steward of the Lord of the Manor ... and that at the last election Joseph Elderton Esq. was bailiff or steward and appointed John Dagge Esq. to be his deputy for the election who was the proper returning officer.

Eventually the House of Commons ruled that the Radnor interest should be upheld. Lord Radnor's steward was the lawfully appointed returning officer. However the lease of the manor of Downton was not sold and Feversham's executors remained the lessees until the Court of Chancery decided that there could be an open sale in 1806. As a result the lease was bought by Jacob earl of Radnor and held in trust for successive Earls until 1875. In that year the Ecclesiastical Commissioners conveyed the reversionary interest to Jacob earl of Radnor and the title of the lordship of the manor has passed with the Radnor title ever since.[7]

The dispute in Downton had arisen due to an unreformed electoral system. Before 1832 fewer than 13% of the adult male population and probably no women could vote in parliamentary elections.[8] As with most constitutional matters in England, the election process had evolved gradually over many centuries and the precise question of who could and who could not vote was largely governed by custom and precedent. There was no legal requirement to register in order to cast a vote but underpinning this right was the belief that only men of property should choose their government, because only property ownership or tenancy at that time signified a respected place in society.

There were two types of constituencies, county and borough, roughly equivalent to rural and town. In Downton and the surrounding area a man could obtain the right to vote by one of two routes. If he owned property outside the boundaries of the borough of Downton worth 40 shillings or more in rent a year, he could vote for a Wiltshire candidate because this was the county qualification. Alternatively if he owned or was a tenant of a burgage property in the borough of Downton this entitled him to vote for a member of parliament to represent Downton borough. The law stated that such a man could vote if he had:

> a freehold interest in burgage tenements held by certain rents, fealty and suit of court [9]

However it was rarely a free vote. As the majority of burgage properties in Downton were owned by two important families, it was they who controlled the elections by persuading their tenants to vote for their chosen candidate. The two Downton MPs were in the pocket of powerful and wealthy property owners. This was increasingly the case in the 17th and 18th centuries and is vividly illustrated by the list of members of parliament for Downton from the early 1600s onwards.

Before this a variety of names appear as Downton MPs with a man rarely representing Downton more than once. From the early 17th century until 1832, when it was disenfranchised, Downton's parliamentary representation was noticeably dominated by a small number of families. Raleigh, Herbert, Bockland and Ashe are names which appear regularly in the 17th century. In the 18th century the Duncombe family name recurs, including Robert Shafto. Towards the end of the century we see an increasing number of Bouveries. Both these families held large estates not just in Wiltshire. They were able to influence electors through deference accorded to them as landlord and sometimes as employer. To vote against their chosen candidate risked losing one's home or job in an age when there was no legal protection for tenant or employee.

The conclusion is that parliamentary representation became more aristocratic over these two centuries eventually leading to resentment and near revolution in the first three decades of the 19th century. In the case of Bouverie versus Duncombe the House of Commons recognised the conveyancing of property for electoral purposes as corrupt and ruled against it in the Radnor claim. It was only a matter of time before the parliamentary electoral system would have to be reformed.

The representation of Downton by two MPs had remained unchanged since the 15th century despite the fact that its population had risen only slightly.[10] Industrialisation in the Midlands and the North was leading to the rapid growth of cities such as Manchester, Liverpool and Sheffield yet the South had greater representation in parliament. There had been massive shifts in population to new industrial towns, resulting in a number of serious anomalies. In 1831, the cities of Manchester, Leeds, Birmingham and Sheffield had not a single MP between them, despite their rapidly increasing populations. Seven miles north of Downton Old Sarum, with no inhabitants at all, returned two MPs. In this context the status of Downton, with its small population sending two MPs to Westminster, seems almost as peculiar.

In addition to the Duncombe-Bouverie dispute, the election to parliament for Downton of Robert Southey in 1826 serves as a powerful illustration of a system urgently in need of reform. Robert Southey, the famous Lakeland poet and Poet Laureate at the time of his election, took a firm stance against industrialisation, preferring the feudal society of medieval England to the fast changing urban society.[11] Southey refused to take his seat when he found that he had been elected as one of Downton's MPs. Without his knowledge, his name had been put forward as a candidate by the earl of Radnor simply because the earl admired views expressed by Southey in his recent book in which he defended the establishment of the Church of England against Catholic Emancipation.[12] Southey was horrified to discover he had been elected for a town about which he knew nothing and he hastily explained to the Speaker of the House that he was unqualified to represent the borough:

> For me to change my scheme of life and go into parliament would
> be to commit a moral and intellectual suicide.

Another electoral anomaly was that one cottage in The Borough carried voting rights even though it had ceased to exist. Number 13 The Borough had been destroyed in the 1670s to allow for the digging of the New Court Carrier, part of the construction of the water meadows by Sir Joseph Ashe, and yet it still retained its voting rights.

Elections were rowdy, public affairs. Voting was by a show of hands in front of the White Horse Inn alongside the village cross and votes

The missing burgage property, number 13 The Borough. The construction of
the New Court Carrier, flowing under Mould's Bridge, seen here, resulted
in the demolition of the cottage, which nevertheless retained its voting right
(Margaret Smith)..

were counted by the returning officer. As in the case of Bouverie
versus Duncombe, it was vital to establish who was the lawfully
appointed returning officer; the chaos can be imagined when the
two rival returning officers counted hands and arrived at different
totals. With wild gesticulations and heckling, elections nearly resulted
in riots. Alcohol and food, conveniently available within the White
Horse, were used by candidates to sway voters. No doubt most could
be persuaded to vote, not only out of loyalty and deference, but also
with the promise of free beer and only a rich man could afford the
bar bill.

How the voters of Downton really felt about the need for reform
can only be guessed. True, they could vote under the current system
and reform might lead to Downton's loss of borough status and
with it their right to vote, but how meaningful was that vote? Any
Downton man who cared to consider the broader issues may well have
recognised the need for reform to the electoral process, particularly as
there was increasing rural poverty in the area caused by the end of the
Napoleonic wars and by the enclosure of agricultural land, which an
unreformed parliament had so far failed to tackle.

The mediaeval system of open field farming survived in the
Downton area until the 19th century and manorial courts dominated
many aspects of rural life, particularly land tenure. However the direct
farming of demesne land and the holding of land in return for labour

services had largely disappeared by the late middle ages due to the fall in population brought about by successive waves of the plague and because direct demesne cultivation was simply too difficult to administer and too time-consuming. Instead the lord preferred rent-paying tenants of whom the majority were known as copyholders, so called because they held a copy of the entry in the manorial court roll which gave them title. Exact rights and customs of tenure varied from manor to manor; in Downton the custom was for 'copyhold of inheritance', guaranteed for a fixed number of heirs. Downton custom also dictated that the youngest son inherited rather than the eldest; this tradition was called 'Borough English'. A fee was paid on entry and a heriot, a kind of duty, was paid at the time of death; these practices were vestiges of the medieval system.[13] Copyhold tenure as a method of tenancy was not abolished until 1922 and before that time it was a very common form of tenure in Downton. For this reason manor courts continued to be held twice a year in Downton in the court house in South Lane. Of these the court baron was the type of court proceeding most regularly used and it had a dual function; to try actions for damages under 40 shillings and to deal with transfer of copyhold land. The court baron opened with the following proclamation:

> Oh yes, oh yes, oh yes! All manner of persons who owe suit and service to the court baron of the lord of the manor now to be holden or who have been summoned to appear at this time and place, draw near and give your attendance. Every man answering

The Court House in South Lane built in 1763. Also known as Borough House, it housed the Grammar Free School from 1679 until 1890.

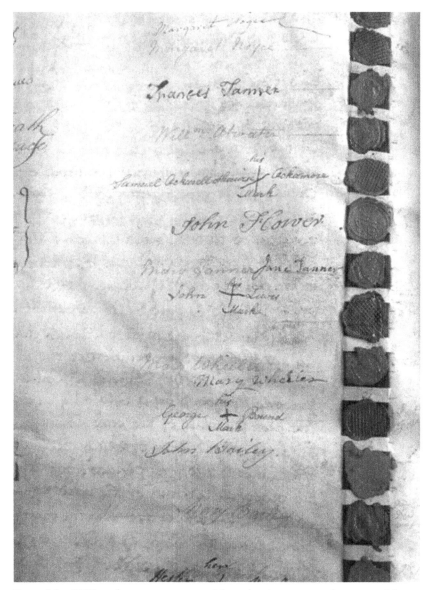

Part of the 1807 enclosure agreement. Note the signatures and crosses of the signatories who could not write. (Radnor papers/ WSA).

to his name when called and thereby saving his amercement.

An example of the proceedings in 1714 involved a widow, Susan Humby, who had inherited a field and a meadow from her brother, Nicholas Bundy. As she was unwilling to hold the land she and her son and heir, Nicholas, surrendered it formally in court to Thomas Lewis and his heirs. Thomas asked to be admitted to the land and as a symbol of the transaction was handed a rod. He paid a fine for entry of nine shillings.[14]

The manor court provided a useful and fair means of local administration, but open field farming largely stifled agricultural innovation and experimentation and meant that subsistence farming was the norm, though it did allow for ancient customs and rights to continue; for example tenants might pasture animals on the common land and in Downton there is specific mention in the ancient customs of tenants' rights to gather wood, turf and furze and to make bricks and mortar from local clay and chalk. These rights often compensated for extremes of poverty and hunger.[15]

In the 17th century there had developed a strong trend towards enclosure of common land and open fields across the country although in many places in South Wiltshire it was affirmed in law relatively late, in the early 1800s.[16] One form of enclosure had already taken place in Downton before that. The development of the water meadows along the Avon valley in Catherine Meadow caused the loss of common land, and many open field holdings had been consolidated by small private enclosure agreements.

Large scale enclosures required an act of parliament. Affecting Downton there were three parliamentary enclosure acts. In 1807 1,600 acres of land between Charlton and Downton were enclosed by agreement between Jacob, earl of Radnor and a number of inhabitants.[17] The agreement apportioning land with its attached map is still in existence. It is typical of such agreements, being very precise and detailed. Altogether 24 villagers were affected.

The document illustrates the issues surrounding enclosure and the effects on the agricultural labourer. The enclosure agreement is signed on each page by three commissioners, Francis Webb of Salisbury, John Bailey of Redlynch and Moses Boorn of Romsey. At the end of the document all parties signed, some with a cross mark signifying their inability to read or write, others with an unpractised hand denoting their slightly better education. The names of the illiterate tenants were recorded by a clerk as Hester Bailey, George Bound, John Lewis and Thomas Ackerell, the latter apparently uncertain of his real name, as he is otherwise known as Ackamore.

How much did the villagers understand what they were signing? Did they feel pressured into signing up for an arrangement which favoured the landlord? Many of the signatories, including the illiterate George Bound received very little land in the new arrangement. George's entry reads:

> Unto and for George Bound one cottage or tenement and garden
> of the said George Bound, containing one rood and ten perches.

This was a very small allotment and not enough to support a family in the days when yields per acre were poor and when the customary rights of tenants such as pasturing animals on common land, were lost. So George Bound would have had to seek additional work to survive. He did at least receive some land where many received none. Poverty and ignorance may have precluded many from claiming their rightful allocation of land post-enclosure.

Enclosure was an expensive business and commissioners and legal experts took months to draw up plans and documents. Often roads and tracks had to be rerouted; in the case of the 1807 agreement two bridleways, four public and two private roads were affected. Enclosed land had to be fenced or hedged. These costs of £2,140 8s. 3d. were shared in 1807 between the eight principal landowners, in other cases it was shared by all.

In 1822 another enclosure act was passed which allotted ninety-four parcels of land, the majority to the Pleydell-Bouveries, Robert Shafto and the Eyres of Newhouse. The third act was in 1847, the bulk again being settled with the Pleydell-Bouveries. When W.H. Hudson recorded the mid-nineteenth century memories of a Wiltshire shepherd in his book, *A Shepherd's Life,* in 1910 he found there was still resentment of enclosure among the rural working classes.

The Downton farm labourer was not helped by a 60% decline in wages in real terms, against the price of bread, between 1795 and 1825.[18] Rural hardship was exacerbated with the ending of the Napoleonic wars in 1815 which brought soldiers back to Britain and contributed to a rise in unemployment. The developing industries in the Midlands and the North, with the introduction of machinery to do a man's work, aggravated the problems of rural Wiltshire. The cotton mills of the North contributed to the decline of Salisbury's woollen cloth trade and spelt the end of fulling mills powered by water. There had been a fulling mill in Downton since medieval times. Threshing machines took work away from farm labourers and the machines and their owners were the targets of the angry unemployed. In the Middle Ages, Wiltshire ranked tenth of the English counties in terms of population. By the mid 19th century it ranked twenty-fourth and by the end of the century twenty-eighth.

A reliance on seasonal agricultural work in the area was an added problem as there was little alternative employment. Some country people, including Downton men, answered with protest. Jill Chambers in her book, *Wiltshire Machine Breakers,* cites an 1811 report by Thomas Davis, steward to the Marquis of Bath, whose estate was at Longleat in Wiltshire:

> It is a melancholy fact that... the labourers of many parts of this county....may be truly said to be at this time in a wretched condition. The dearness of provision, the scarcity of fuel and above all the failure of spinning work for the women and children have put it almost out of the power of the village poor to live by their industry.

In 1826 William Cobbett reported much the same picture in his *Rural Rides* and Wiltshire farm workers were the lowest paid in England even if they could find work.

This increasing impoverishment and dispossession of the agricultural working classes led to the so-called Swing Riots. They began in Kent in August 1830, sparked by two previous poor harvests and by the end of the year had spread to most southern counties. The disturbances took various forms. There were threatening letters to landowners from 'Captain Swing' who may or may not have existed, threshing machines were attacked, property was vandalised and burned and there were riotous assemblies. The targets were landowners and poor law overseers who had the authority to administer workhouses and poor relief funds. In Wiltshire the poor had particular cause to complain because the county awarded the smallest bread allowance by way of poor relief compared to anywhere else in the country. The authorities struggled to maintain adequate poor relief because of the sheer numbers of destitute families and this was exacerbated by a new system of relief known as the Speenhamland system whereby parishes could supplement low wages. This often had the unintended effect of tempting employers to pay their workers less.[19]

There were a number of incidents of Swing Riots in Fordingbridge and a serious riot targeting the home of John Benett MP at Tisbury, resulting in one death. There was one recorded incident in Downton, a riot which took place at New Court Farm. The farm was then on the main thoroughfare running north and south through the village and therefore it would have been relatively easy to assemble protesters by word of mouth. Several Downton men were among those arrested and brought to trial.

Many of the Downton protesters were sentenced to transportation to Australia. They included Charles Bennett, Thomas Gange, Charles Hayter, William Hayter, Barnabas Hutchinson, John Newman, Edward Nutbean, Samuel Quinton, Charles Shepherd, John Slade, George Webb, William Webb and John Weeks. Not all were agricultural labourers. Quinton was a barber and wig maker. He was 26 years old and described in court records as having a ruddy, freckled

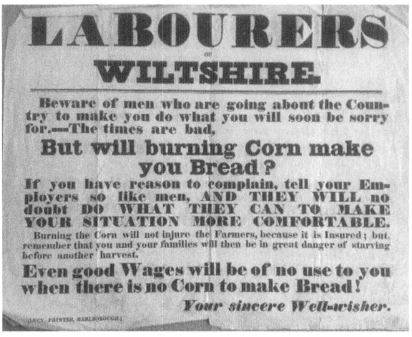

A leaflet aimed at dissuading disaffected labourers in Wiltshire from joining the Swing Rioters.(WSA).

complexion.[20] He had no previous convictions but he was given a life sentence and delivered by 'special gaol delivery' to the ship *Eleanor* in Southampton and thence to the penal colony of New South Wales in Australia. Newman, Shepherd, Weeks, Slade and the two Webb brothers were also given life sentences and were transported by the *Eliza* to Van Diemen's Land (now Tasmania). Like Quinton, they were regarded as dangerous and their delivery to Southampton docks was by the same method. Hayter and Hutchinson also sailed on the *Eliza* to Van Diemen's Land but were each sentenced to seven years.[21] Some of the surnames listed here still survive in Downton.

The trials took place in Salisbury and were reported nationally. *The Times* described the scene outside the court house as the prisoners were taken away after sentencing:

> The cart to remove the prisoners ... was surrounded by bewildered relatives of the convicted prisoners. The weeping and wailing of the different parties as they pressed the hands of the convicts as they stepped into the cart, was truly heartrending. We never saw so distressing a spectacle.[22]

Another of the Downton inhabitants sentenced was Silas Webb. The Court records reveal that he was eighteen years old and that he:

> assembled with other persons and destroyed a threshing machine, the property of James Shelley, at Downton.

He was described by his master as being 'not very bad'. He was very young and because his master spoke up for him he was not transported but received a three month prison sentence which he served in Devizes Prison. One can imagine this young man being caught up in the drama of the moment at New Court Farm and persuaded to commit a crime which was uncharacteristic of his normal behaviour.[23]

The Swing Riots were not political in aim but rather were rooted in need and hunger. William Cobbett famously defied anyone to 'agitate a fellow on a full stomach'. Establishment figures nevertheless saw them as a threat to stable society and government at a time when the horrors of the French Revolution were within recent memory. In July 1830 the anti-reformist French king, Charles X was overthrown. The sometimes violent acts of the Wessex rick burners, and other physical threats against the lives of public figures, including the Duke of Wellington, were a persuasive factor when MPs voted for the Great Reform Act of 1832. Agricultural workers were regarded as the most docile of the working classes. In the 1830s their riotous behaviour suggested that the country was close to revolution and many members of the establishment came round to supporting electoral reform for reasons of self-preservation. The earl of Radnor who succeeded his father in 1828, was one of those in favour. His younger brother the Honourable Philip Pleydell-Bouverie also supported reform and agreed to stand for election in Downton in 1831, knowing that his seat was in jeopardy should the Reform Bill succeed. His views were summed up in a speech he made in Malmesbury in 1831 and appear genuine:

> I came forward to afford you the opportunity of sending to Parliament two Members pledged to a defined plan of reform; I was willing to bind myself to that plan, because I thought its provisions just and reasonable – a plan which will give to the middling, intelligent, independent classes the power of selecting such persons to represent them and their interests, and to manage their affairs, as they approve.[24]

Pleydell-Bouverie, like most reform bill supporters of the day, specified that the vote should be given to the skilled and educated middle classes. His speech in no way suggests that farm labourers and other manual workers like those involved in rioting should receive the vote. Pro-reformers like Pleydell-Bouverie hoped to avert revolution by drawing the middle classes away from radicalism.

In that year he became Downton's last MP. It is interesting to note that his father, then Viscount Folkestone, had contributed to the notorious Downton electoral dispute in the late 18th century described earlier in this chapter. That dispute highlighted corrupt elections in small boroughs, a fact which cannot have escaped the Honourable Philip Pleydell-Bouverie. An irony of history is that the Great Reform Act, with its aim of enfranchising more men in a fair and consistent manner, disenfranchised Downton completely, removing the vote from some of its inhabitants and abolishing the borough's right to send two MPs to Westminster.

There were lengthy and heated debates in parliament over the details of electoral reform and these included consideration of exactly which boroughs should be disenfranchised. The decision was loosely based on the population of a borough in 1821. This was the most recent year for which precise figures were available as the results of the 1831 census were not yet published. In Downton the calculation was complicated by the fact that the boundaries of the borough were not recorded and also because there were a number of men entitled to vote who lived outside the strict confines of the borough. A survey was conducted in 1831 and the overseer of the parish, George Mannings, stated that the population of the parish was 3,961 of which 264 were ratepayers. The figures seem excessive and are slightly misleading because he included 19 'other farm houses', presumably to strengthen the case for maintaining borough status. In an accompanying note, Mannings argued that Downton 'is rapidly increasing in population ... and is therefore fully capable of forming a constituency'.[25] But his evidence was not robust enough to convince the Home Office to maintain Downton's borough status.

On 7th June 1832 the Great Reform Bill received the Royal Assent. The Duke of Wellington said gloomily that, 'The government of England is destroyed' but there were rejoicings countrywide.[26] Locally the *Salisbury Journal* reported that,

> A new era commences in the history of the country. The suppression of the nomination boroughs and the substitution of the constituency of great and populous towns for those mockeries of representation, of which corruption knew everything and the

constitution nothing, will alone, without reference to any other provisions of the bill, work a great change.[27]

One medal cast to commemorate the event stated:

OLD SARUM DESERTED IN THE YEAR 1217 – DISENFRANCHISED JUNE 7th 1832

Downton was disenfranchised. It was one of 56 boroughs which lost the right to send two MPs to parliament and therefore it ceased to be a borough, in other words the town became a village. As a whole Wiltshire lost 16 MPs, the number shrinking from 34 to 18. Anyone still entitled to vote under the county constituency rules needed to travel to Salisbury to vote, as it was the nearest polling station for South Wiltshire.

Despite great optimism, the Great Reform Act did not markedly change the composition of parliament, although it was the precursor of much more widespread electoral reform in years to come. For the moment the right to vote was given to the urban middle classes who allied with the aristocracy in their aspirations. Governments continued to be aristocratic by nature. [28] The open ballot system remained in force until 1872 meaning voters could still be influenced. But the days of heckling and buying a beer for the good men of Downton at the White Horse, to persuade them to vote in a certain way, were gone for ever.

A Downton family in the 1880s; the Weeks (author's collection).

7

Wider Horizons

The period from the 1832 Reform Act to the early 20th century was a time of mixed fortunes for Downton, as the community adapted to its change of status. In 1841 the census recorded the population of Downton as 3,648.[1] If the figure is to be trusted it is a slight increase from 1831, a trend which continued for two decades. After the 1851 census the population fell until the end of the century in common with much of rural Wiltshire, a change brought about largely by a move away from a rural economy, coupled with an agricultural depression and the expansion of industry and urban life in towns such as Southampton.[2] To this one must add the demise of hand lacemaking in the village.

The disenfranchisement of the borough in 1832 resulted in a bizarre political scandal. A Mr. Hobbs, the mayor of Downton at the time, was asked to hand over the Downton mace to the lord of the manor, at the request of the manor court. The mayor was originally responsible for law and order but his functions in Downton were largely ceremonial by 1832, the duties having been superseded by local constables and justices of the peace.[3] A local saying sarcastically suggested that one of the few functions of the mayor was, 'when he saw three pigs wallowing in the mud in The Borough he had the right to whip up the middle one and lay down in its place.'[4]

Hobbs refused to hand over the mace, it is said because the correct papers could not be produced, and he took the mace with him when he moved to Southampton into a house which he later named Mace Cottage. The story was recounted by A.R. Woodford who collected various episodes from Downton's past and although some of Woodford's research might be conjecture this particular story is substantiated by the fact the 6th earl of Radnor purchased the mace for Downton in 1921 from a pawnbroker's shop in Southampton and frequently repeated the story.[5]

The Downton mace was made in London by Gabriel Sleath in 1714 and was probably given to the village by Sir Charles Duncombe or his heir and John Eyre, who were Downton's MPs from 1705 to 1711. It bears the arms of the Duncombe family and the chevron of the Eyre family. That these two families included their own coats of arms on a symbol of authority bequeathed to Downton tells us that they were confident of their families' influence in Downton in the early 18th century.[6]

Emigration

In the 1830s Downton witnessed a government experiment in social engineering. The 1834 Poor Law Amendment Act allowed parishes to raise funds for emigration and in 1835 Downton's select vestry[7] sponsored the emigration of 25 men and women to Ontario, Canada.[8] The plan was in part a response to the Swing Riots and demonstrated perhaps less a humanitarian concern for the distress of working class families and more a desire to lower the poor rate. The limited opportunities available to the rural poor, who relied much on irregular seasonal work, were regarded as burdensome by poor law guardians. In Downton the decline of the hand-made lace industry had created further difficulties. The list of emigrants who took up the offer of a new life across the Atlantic includes members of several old Downton families and also Silas Webb, the young man who had been convicted of taking part in a riot at New Court Farm in 1830. He had served his sentence but no doubt felt that there was little future in Downton. The group of emigrants spent five nights at the Quebec Hotel in Portsmouth, awaiting good weather before their Atlantic crossing aboard the *Louisa*. During that time they were treated to substantial quantities of food and drink, including ale, port, lobster and steak.

Little is known of their fate in the New World but according to the description of a similar group from Frome by William Lyon Mackenzie, a prominent Canadian politician:

> They were poor but in general fine looking people and such as I was glad to see come to America. It is my opinion that few among them will ever forget being cooped up below deck for four weeks.

When an announcement was made in February the following year, for all interested parties, namely fathers of families and single persons to attend a meeting about a further possible emigration it was well attended, despite the fact that several passengers had perished on similar voyages from other locations. The second party sailed on the *King William* on April 7th 1836.[9]

Altogether about 220 people left Downton.[10] It was the biggest government sponsored emigration project in England that year and provides an insight into the extent of rural poverty in this part of England. The minutes of the Alderbury Poor Law Union (by this time the poor law in Downton was administered by neighbouring Alderbury) contains an application to buy shoes for some of the migrants:

> 25 pairs of men's shoes, 100 girls and boys shoes from 3 to 15 years and 25 pairs of women's shoes for the care of the poor about to emigrate from Downton.

The parish raised a portion of the money for the journey and support for the migrants also came from a government loan on which Lord Radnor paid the interest. It was clear that the relief of the poor had reached crisis point as the Alderbury Poor Law Union relief rose from £3,423 paid out in 1834 to £3,771 in 1835.

The Downton migrants were fortunate in having a good ship's captain, George Thomas, for they arrived safely in Quebec on May 28th. The subsequent lives of most of them are largely unrecorded, although James Chalke and John Pracey later appeared in the records of the Talbot settlement on the shores of Lake Eerie. Irish born Colonel Thomas Talbot had persuaded the British government to help him set up a settlement in virgin wilderness and each family was granted 200 acres of which 50 were in perpetuity. Colonel Talbot had a reputation as a tough and uncompromising man who chose his settlers personally and who did not hesitate to take land back from them if they failed to abide by his rules. He was able to do this because he entered their names in the land registry in pencil and would rub out those who crossed him.[11] Life would have been very hard for the settlers, with the clearance of thick and mature woodlands and the ploughing of virgin soil the first requirement.

We know that at least four families, the Champs, the Biddlecombes, the Forders and the Moodys, returned home as their names turn up in later parish records.[12] It is thought that the death of a daughter in Canada was the reason for the return of the Champs though their change of heart may have been something of an exception among migrants. Despite its harshness, many viewed their new life positively, if with a tinge of home-sickness, as can be seen from this letter sent to the Vicar of Downton:

> This I have to say, that any labouring man can live better by working three days a week than at home by working all the week. But should any think of coming, I would first advise them to lay it to heart whether they can wean their hearts from the old country first, not to reflect after. Many are so weak-minded as to think they are going to be sold as slaves.
>
> But I can certify that this is the place for liberty. Here are no poor rates for there are no poor here. There is plenty of deer and wild turkeys and pheasants and game free from anyone. But I don't trouble about it at present for it pays me better to get to work and there are many that do.
>
> Please to tell Mrs. Roberts that if they were here, they would get plenty of places for her girls. They are very much attached to English girls and get a dollar a week for them. Please to tell William Chalke that brick making is good here. Should any think of coming, tell them to come away by the beginning of March, as they will have the summer before them. But as to the state of the country it is a fine country and very healthy. Lace sells well here too.[13]

One of the oldest photographs of Downton is this one of number 59 The Borough, with, it is thought John Weeks, and his wife Eliza standing outside. c.1880. Note the burgage numbers above the doors (author's collection).

The reference to game is particularly interesting as Beryl Hurley in her unpublished work *Rough Justice*[14] states that conviction under the game laws accounted for 23% of all petty crime in Wiltshire between 1821 and 1830. Landowners (who commonly served as the judiciary) saw it as a growing problem and as a consequence penalties were increased over time and by 1803 were extremely severe. A first offence often brought imprisonment. Subsequent offences could entail hard labour, whipping or transportation. Justices of the Peace were also regularly convicting Downton people for stealing food other than game, mothers stealing turnips and young boys taking apples are just two examples in the records. In 1830 three Downton boys, George Alexander, Michael Futcher and Ephraim Bundy, received a sentence of a month's imprisonment for stealing apples. The report that there were 'plenty of deer and wild turkeys and pheasants and game free from anyone' in Canada would have had considerable appeal. It is surely no coincidence that Michael Futcher and George Alexander are to be found in the manifest of the *King William* sailing for a new life in Canada in 1836.

A view of Victorian Downton

The censuses of 1851 and 1861 recorded that Downton's population decreased from 3,848 to 3,566. Even more striking is a comparison of the occupations of many Downton women. In 1851 there were 18 lacemakers in The Borough, nearly all of them the wives and daughters of agricultural labourers. One, Louisa Chalke, was only 13 years old. Some households were home to several lacemakers. For example at No. 17 The Borough lived Jacob Arney, farm labourer, his wife Jane, a lacemaker, their daughter Anne Moody, also a lacemaker and her husband John Moody, a farm labourer. Both Anne and John were middle-aged and presumably unable to maintain their own home. Two grandchildren also lived under the same roof. By 1861 the census enumerator recorded only one lacemaker and one former lacemaker in the whole of The Borough. The village's cottage industry was squeezed out by mechanisation. Home industries such as lacemaking had been a useful fall back income where agricultural labourers were paid by the day and frequently laid off in slack times. But by the second half of the nineteenth century men sought work elsewhere as wages were far higher in a factory. The drift away from rural life was in progress.

Many of the thatched cottages along the village greens changed little in external appearance over hundreds of years, and some would survive into the twentieth century. From 1831 street lighting was introduced consisting of oil lamps including one attached to The

Borough cross, lit by a street lighter. These survived until just after the First World War. Some cottages had been rebuilt and repaired beyond recognition since the Middle Ages and in Victorian times thatch was often replaced with tile; a typical example of which is the cottage now known as *Dormers* on the south side of the western village green. Downton had its own brickworks in Moot Lane and most older properties in the village were constructed from this local source of building material. Nearly all Borough cottages retained long plots behind, which were prized as orchards and kitchen gardens.

Typically in the mid to late 19th century cottages in Downton contained only two rooms on the ground floor; one housed a range, fuelled by wood or coal and provided the only source of heat and cooking facilities. In winter it was cosy but drying laundry was usually draped around it. The bedrooms above were usually interconnected, with nothing in the way of an upstairs landing, so affording little privacy. There was no electricity; lighting was by candle and oil lamp. A well in the garden provided water. There was no provision for bathing in privacy. A wash down at the kitchen sink had to suffice with the occasional treat of a tin bath filled with water heated on the range. Few properties had inside toilets. Usually these were at the bottom of the garden in a small shed and consisted of a bucket fitted with a wooden seat. Waste was usually buried in the garden or thrown into the river. The water quality suffered although the Avon was never seriously polluted, even though many villagers did not regard it as a place of beauty and pleasure as people do today. Cottages with gardens by the river had their privies conveniently sited as close to the river bank as possible for easy disposal.[15]

Thatched cottages, now demolished, which stood at the junction of Wick Lane and Salisbury Road (Margaret Smith).

Borough Cottages (Margaret Smith)..

Many cottages still had earth floors and no damp courses. Damp houses contributed to lung disease and the absence of sanitation was another danger to health. Although a measure of immunity could be developed by adulthood it was the youngest who were most usually affected. Parish registers and parish magazines reveal that on average there was one infant death in Downton every month so there was every chance of families losing babies, toddlers and older children. The 1885 Downton parish magazine records that the Swatridge family lost two daughters, one aged 16 in January and one aged 6 in February. In the same year a little boy Henry Charles Wort died. He was about three years old but his exact date of birth is unknown, even though registration of births was compulsory after 1874. His mother was listed but not the name of his father and so he was probably illegitimate. In Victorian England the most common cause of child and infant mortality was diarrhoea, though cause of death was rarely given in the records of infants so one can only surmise. Successive governments recognised the problem of waste disposal and clean water resulting in a series of Public Health Acts (1848, 1872 and 1875) but the regulations were rarely enforced in villages such as Downton until the 20th century.

Fortunately Downton was never hit by the cholera epidemic[16] which spread through the slums of Victorian industrial towns and cities, but it was clearly feared by the local authorities. In the 1830s Downton's select vestry had made exhaustive preparations should an

The High Street looking towards the mills, before the building of the present tannery (Margaret Smith)..

outbreak occur. These included the setting up of a temporary hospital at a distance from the village. There was provision for help with fuel, clothing and bedding for the sick and all inhabitants had to remove from their dwellings 'filth of every description, particularly dung and ashes, to cleanse their drains and privies and to burn all decayed articles of rubbish'.[17]

The village greens remained a distinctive feature of Downton and were never built on apart from one additional house sited at the western end facing eastwards, in the early part of the 19th century. In Victorian times the village pound opposite the present day Memorial Hall was used to keep stray animals, which were rounded up by the village hayward and kept for owners to claim. The Memorial Hall, built in 1840, dominated the lower end of The Borough. The portico was added later and it was not initially a public hall but a boys' school for non-conformists. Known as the British School it was built on land donated by the earl of Radnor. By 1857 it had 88 pupils and was regarded as a 'model of good management and efficiency'. There was a girls' school at the lower end of The Borough.[18] The village cross was in a rather sorry state until it was repaired in 1897. It had stood at the ancient crossroads of the village probably since at least the 14th century. The White Horse Inn was perhaps quieter than in earlier times, no longer the venue of fiercely contested elections by show of hands. To the north Gravel Close had a few thatched cottages along its way, as did South Lane in which the Court House and the Baptist Chapel were situated.

There was a parish workhouse on the corner of The Borough and Green Lane which had been in use since 1731.[19] Cottages were sited behind it, along Green Lane. These were demolished in the 20th century to make way for industrial buildings.[20] Nearby, Catherine Bridge had been newly rebuilt in 1820 but was without the footpath it bears today. In the old High Street, the tannery and mills operated alongside the leet, although the tannery building was not the one we see today.

St. Laurence Church underwent extensive renovation in 1859-60. This involved taking down the tower which had been raised in 1791 so that Lord Radnor could see it from Longford Castle. The additional weight had caused structural problems. The four pinnacles, one at each corner of the tower, were retained when the tower was lowered. Interior work was also carried out, including the removal of a partition between the chancel and the nave. Oak panelling was taken away and the Ten Commandments, a textual record, may have been painted above the nave at this time by a local artist.

Work began on the construction of the Salisbury to West Moors railway line through Downton in 1863 and was completed in 1866. During the construction period the population was swollen by gangs of workers who were drafted in. The station was situated to the north of the eastern end of the High Street, necessitating a bridge to carry the railway over the road at Lode Hill. Although the railway was mainly used for the transport of agricultural produce, it had a social impact as well, enabling faster and more convenient travel to Salisbury. A few Downton boys travelled daily on the railway to attend

Lode Hill and the railway bridge (Margaret Smith)..

A horse and cart outside Hickman's shop in the High Street. More recently until 2014 this was a newsagent's shop (Margaret Smith)..

Bishop Wordsworth's Grammar School in Salisbury. For the first time families with a little cash to spare could venture as far as Weymouth or Bournemouth for a seaside break, something impossible for their forebears.[21]

Jones the Butcher at what is now the pinch point at the eastern end of The Borough (Margaret Smith)..

106

The old post office in the High Street (Margaret Smith)..

The railway may have opened the village to outside influences but in many respects Downton remained self-supporting and there was little need to venture out of the village for everyday goods and services. Trade directories provide a snapshot of the working and commercial life of Downton mid-century, clearly demonstrating how much was on offer. Some tradesmen such as clockmakers and maltsters who had been in the village in the 18th century were no longer listed in Kelly's Trade Directory by the mid-19th century while several leather workers were still present, as they had been for centuries. A lady could buy a dress, a straw bonnet, gloves and shoes in Downton and a gentleman could have his horse shod, saddled and harnessed. Shopkeepers must have kept long hours because by 1893 it was announced in the parish magazine that shops would close at 8pm, except on Wednesdays from May to September when they would close at 5pm.... 'We feel sure that customers will be willing to assist in carrying out this scheme as it seems that a very hard working and obliging portion of our community should have opportunity for rest and recreation.' A Victorian shop front, formerly Steven's of Downton, a draper and general outfitter, is preserved and displayed in Breamore Countryside Museum. It was removed to convert 101 The Borough into a residential property in 1985.

There were at least six public houses, the White Horse Inn, the Three Horse Shoes (now Horseshoe Court), the Free and Easy (now

81 The Borough), the George and Dragon (now Dragon House), the New Inn (now the Wooden Spoon) and the King's Arms. There was a post office but no bank. Two fairs were still held, mainly for horses and sheep in April and October, but the directory recites that the market had long disappeared, the nearest being in Salisbury. For this reason three carriers offered their services to take people and goods to Salisbury on Tuesdays, Thursdays and Saturdays. They were Richard Roles, George Bundy and Eliza Snelgrove. Two more coach and horse services were available, Henry Read on Thursdays to Southampton and Richard Quinton to Romsey once a week. The pick-up point for all of them was 'their dwelling'.[22]

There was an active temperance society and some adult opportunities for self-improvement, in bible classes and courses run by the authorities to teach better food production. The county council offered free courses on butter making to anyone with two or more cows. The impression is of a village of hard-working and God fearing inhabitants.

Education

For the vast majority of young people born into modest Downton families in the middle of the nineteenth century, career prospects were limited, though a little better than in earlier times, owing to a number of local schools. Downton had been fortunate in its connection with Winchester College since the Middle Ages, giving a

Downton school girls in the High Street, late 19th century (Margaret Smith)..

Downton school pupils at the turn of the century (author's collection).

small number of talented and hard working boys the chance to receive an education in the famous school. These boys were encouraged to enter the priesthood. In 1679, quite unusually, Downton had also been endowed with its own school, the Grammar Free School, held in the Court House in South Lane, for the instruction of twelve village boys. Most were the sons of freeholders. The school was established by two of Downton's MPs, Sir Joseph Ashe and Gyles Eyre. An issue which no doubt escaped the notice of the village at the time was that Gyles Eyre's wealth came from a fortune made in the West Indies, which included profits from slavery. Additional funds came from the profits of the two village fairs. The school survived until 1890 but it was always short of money because the annual net income from the fairs was never more than £9. The number of pupils never exceeded twenty; they were educated for up to three years. How much of a difference this limited education made to the prospects of its pupils is hard to say.

In the mid-nineteenth century there was no universal state provision for education. There were 36 so called day schools in Downton but they were not teaching the three Rs and were simply small scale apprenticeship establishments teaching trades and crafts such as lacemaking.[23] Many might be regarded now as sweat shops.

The Downton Board School building, now Downton Primary School.

In the early 1830s the vicar, Liscombe Clarke, concerned about the lack of girls' education, started a girls' school. By 1833 47 girls attended the school in Barford Lane, managed by his wife who enlarged it in 1850. By 1857 it had 90-100 pupils, remarkable for a building of modest size.[24]

Despite a generous school provision, literacy was not universal. For example one village girl, Eliza Prince, could not sign her name on her marriage certificate when she married John Weeks in 1863 and instead signed with a cross. Child labour was widespread in agricultural communities and was not just associated with industry and mining. Often it must have interrupted education.

A substantial development affecting every girl and boy in Downton was the opening of a board school in 1896 in Gravel Close. The 1870 Education Act required communities to make arrangements for state education by electing a school board wherever there was inadequate provision. Education became compulsory for all children between the ages of five and twelve in 1880. The first headmaster of Downton's new board school was John George Northover who had been the last headmaster of the British School. The school building was surmounted with a belfry to summon the children and is a fine example of a Victorian board school. It still houses Downton Primary School.[25] Learning was usually by rote with a strong focus on literacy. All school subjects were taught with confidence typical of the Victorian period. This was a society in which the majority of people felt assured of Britain's important role in the wider world. The world map on the classroom wall displayed in pink the extent of the British Empire and children were taught the United Kingdom's global influence. In history they learnt the steady progress of democracy since medieval times. They were taught loyalty to Queen and country, attendance at church and obedience to elders and betters. There was little opportunity to question or debate; facts were learnt dutifully with a certain amount of fear and trepidation.

Towards the end of the century the Downton Agricultural College provided specialised further education in the area, but not specifically for local boys. It was founded in 1880 by Professor Wrightson, who had gained a reputation as a professor of agriculture at Cirencester College. The Downton Agricultural College was situated just outside the parish boundary at South Charford Manor. Students were recruited from all over the country yet the College provided work for a number of villagers, bringing a local economic upturn as most of the students were lodged with villagers. Professor and Mrs. Wrightson were active citizens who played an influential role in Downton. The Professor taught at the Downton Board School and was a churchwarden. His large family of eleven children, including a son named Cerdic, occupied a house in the High Street called *The Warren*. The Wrightsons held sports days and garden parties, providing entertainment for local people, in the grounds of the College. On several occasions Mrs. Wrightson organised for the village children to be taken by horse and cart to the College where games were laid on for them.

On 3rd June 1884 Professor Wrightson, his son and forty of his students were the first on the scene when the Downton to Fordingbridge train was derailed in a serious accident.[26] The Wrightsons were also unwittingly responsible for putting Downton on the map over a hundred years later for a very different reason, when the actor and writer, Julian Fellowes, now Lord Fellowes of West Stafford, named his television costume drama *Downton Abbey* on account of his lineage from the Professor and his wife.[27] Oddly Wrightson is also attributed as one of the first people in the country to participate in surfing. In 1890 he was introduced to the sport, normally thought to have been brought to England in the 1960s, by two Hawaiian Princes, David and Jonah Kawanaankoa, who were his students at the College. They wrote home to say that:

> Even Wrightson is learning surf riding and will be able to ride as
> well as we in a few days more. He likes this very much for it is a
> very good sport.[28]

The Wrightsons were not the only gentlefolk in Downton with a
sense of social responsibility. There are references in parish magazines
of the later 19th century to the vigorous work of 3rd Earl Nelson,
who was a descendant of Admiral Lord Nelson's brother and who
lived at Trafalgar House.[29] Mr. Elias Pitt Squarey of Moot House also
contributed to village life. Both made charitable donations to villagers
in need, particularly to victims of flooding, and both were major donors
when the church needed repair. The garden of Moot House, the site
of King Stephen's castle, was regularly used to stage festivals, fetes and
celebrations and then as now, the villagers of Downton enthusiastically
involved themselves in the merry-making.

In the 1880s the parish magazine passed this comment:

> The Downton of old is not the Downton of today ... Downton
> has generally settled into a quiet, hum-drum, respectable village,
> little dreaming of royal visits, vigorous election contests and a
> country squire important enough to oppose the hale and generous
> house of Radnor.

The reference to royal visits probably refers to the supposed visit
of Queen Elizabeth I, and the vigorous election contests hint at the
Duncombe - Bouverie dispute. The article also obliquely refers to the
effect not only of the 1832 Reform Act but also the Ballot Act, which
was passed in 1872 by Gladstone's government. The new law went
a long way to ensuring that the aristocracy could no longer control
parliament. Also in 1884 in rural areas male householders and £10
tenants were given the right to vote in general elections, although
surprisingly no comment is passed in the parish magazine. This
together with an earlier law of 1867, relating to male householders in
towns, effectively gave the majority of men in England the vote and
it returned the franchise to men in Downton who had lost it in 1832,
if still alive.

The Local Government Act of 1894 led to the establishment of
Downton's first parish council replacing the select vestry. The parish
council was elected in December 1894 and first met in 1895. Women
ratepayers were now permitted to vote. Although they had been able
to vote in local elections since the Municipal Franchise Act of 1869
there had been legal challenges regarding the rights of married women,
who had at that time no legal identity separate from their husbands.
The Local Government Act of 1894 awarded women the vote in

local elections, regardless of marital status and provided a compelling argument for the national women's suffrage movement.

Agricultural labourers in Downton had experienced hard times since the acts of enclosure despite the fact that this was an age of significant agricultural improvements. It was the more prosperous farmers and landowners who had benefited from enclosure and were able to experiment with new farming techniques. In Downton lived one of the county's best known agricultural innovators in the person of Elias Pitt Squarey (1823 - 1911) of Moot House. Squarey had studied under R. Rawlence, a prizewinning breeder of sheep, and had farmed on a very large scale at Odstock. He also helped to found the Land Loan and Enfranchisement Company which lent money to landlords wanting to improve their land. The *Victoria County History* names him as one of Wiltshire's outstanding innovators but also notes that in south Wiltshire there was little genuine innovation or improvement in farming due to conservatism, challenging market conditions and the poverty of ordinary Wiltshire men.

At the very end of the 19th century a small number of Downton men were involved in the Boer Wars. The First Boer War (1880-81) had come to an end when Gladstone granted the Boers in South Africa their independence. The Second Boer War was a far more drawn out and troubled affair and the second battalion of the Wiltshire regiment was deployed to South Africa and fought in all the major military actions. As far as research reveals, only one Downton

The village square at the turn of the century (Margaret Smith)..

man was killed. Percy Woodford lost his life in a railway accident at Barberton in March 1902 and he is commemorated on a wall plaque in St. Laurence Church. There was no conscription for this colonial war and the effects were felt far less than the great conflicts of the twentieth century. The brother of Mrs. Elias Pitt Squarey of Moot House, General Sir Charles Tucker, served as a senior commander and successfully garrisoned Pretoria. Two Downton couples received the sum of £5 sent personally by Queen Victoria, because they each had four sons serving in the British Army during the conflict.

It was the children born at the end of the 19th century who would witness the horrors of the Great War. Born in the final years of the reign of Queen Victoria into a modest and quiet rural community, they could not have conceived how cataclysmic the changes would be to their world in adulthood.

Queen Victoria died on 22nd January 1901 at Osborne House on the Isle of Wight and many felt they were witnessing the end of an era when her funeral took place the next month. The following year Earl Nelson invited the villagers to a celebration held at Trafalgar House to mark the coronation of Edward VII. A somewhat reduced garden party went ahead in spite of the postponement of the coronation.[30]

An event which had a greater effect locally was the closure of Professor Wrightson's Agricultural College in 1906. Professor Wrightson's second in command, Dr. William Fream, died in that year and Wrightson decided to close the College to concentrate on research and writing. Another loss to the village was the death of Emily Whitchurch who was a member of the Baptist congregation. She became a missionary in China at the turn of the century and perished in the Boxer rebellion in 1900.

The nation was to witness another royal funeral before the outbreak of hostilities in 1914, that of the old King Edward VII, who had spent most of his life as monarch in waiting. Despite his mother's grave doubts he turned out to be a competent and popular king. One of his lasting achievements had been to smooth negotiations with the French, which led to the signing of an Anglo-French entente in 1904. But as Downton marked his funeral in 1910 and celebrated the coronation of George V, little did anyone know that the village sons would soon be called upon under the terms of that treaty to defend France against a German invasion.

War was declared on 4th August 1914.

8

Peace & War

In Downton at the turn of the 20th century life continued to be challenging for rural workers, with a fear of unemployment caused by agricultural mechanisation and New World competition from meat and grain sales. There was the possibility of work at the Downton tan yard which was extended in the early 1900s on the site where hides had been turned into leather since medieval times. Downton produced high quality leather for saddlery and for the soles of shoes.[1] In 1902 the Countess of Radnor opened premises for Downton Home Industries on the site of the old workhouse. This enterprise, intended to provide

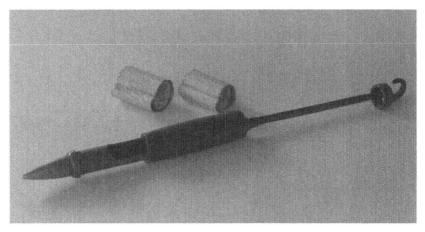

A boot hook concealing a love note, hand made by Albert Futcher and dropped into his girlfriend Katherine Austin's garden from an airship during the First World War.

part time work for local people, gave a welcome boost to Downton's economy. Also welcome, in 1909 the Liberal government introduced an old age pension and a state insurance scheme for the sick. 'God bless Lloyd George' [2] was a common cry among the poorer sections of society who could now draw on basic state support. However cottages still had no electricity; candles and oil lamps were usually the only form of lighting and the bucket toilet at the bottom of the garden remained a common feature.

The largest landowner, the earl of Radnor still owned most cottages in The Borough. Few were inhabited by owner-occupiers. A bailiff, appointed from the village, looked after the Earl's interests as his predecessors had done since the previous century.[3] His duties, which are listed below, were considerably fewer than those of his predecessors, not least because he no longer acted as a returning officer in elections.

> Your duties as bailiff will consist of seeing that the shows on the Green on Fair days are conducted in an orderly manner and you will be entitled to charge by the authority of His Lordship as Lord of the Manor the customary charges of two shillings for each large stall and one shilling for each small stall on the Green at each Fair. You may from time to time be required as Bailiff to serve notices on tenants of the Manor in the event of forfeiture of their land arising, as the duty has always been performed by the Bailiff. In that case special instruction will be given to you by Mr. Coxe, the Steward; but for the present you may consider that your duties as

Downton Home Industries (Margaret Smith).

Workers at Downton Tan Yard, early 20th century (author's collection)..

bailiff will be confined to looking after the Shows as explained above.

In the second decade of the 20th century the gathering European crisis became a cause for concern. When war finally came in August 1914 few could have guessed how it would be fought or how long it would last. Downton men and boys volunteered for the armed services willingly along with neighbours, work colleagues and school friends. Britain had not been involved in a major European war for a century. A hundred years after the Battle of Waterloo weapons of mass destruction were poised for use by the leading European nations, heavy artillery and the machine guns among them. As the spectre of war drew closer, the commanders of armies were aware of their destructive power but the farm boys and tannery workers of Downton were in all probability ignorant of the current technology of war. Little did they know that their commanders would be, in the words of Winston Churchill, 'content to meet machine-gun bullets with the breasts of gallant men'.

For the tannery workers who toiled in a stinking environment the war was a chance to join their comrades and serve in their local regiments. For the sons of generations of farm workers, who had suffered the worst pay in the country and who were subject to sporadic unemployment, this was an opportunity to get regular and reasonable wages. There was no evidence in 1914 of the feisty rebelliousness which some Downton men had shown in the past. There were no demonstrations against the declaration of war, instead there was conformity and a desire to fight alongside one's peers. Volunteer soldiers and regulars posed proudly for the camera ready to fight for King and Country. The war against the central powers of Germany, Austria-Hungary and Turkey, was a cause they believed in by offering support to Britain's allies, chiefly France, Russia and 'Brave Little Belgium'.[4] The view of the Great War as a pointless and futile conflict was almost unknown at the time. The current public perception has superimposed that interpretation on the era with hindsight. It is a view which came about only when peace was lost in the 1930s but certainly not in the early years of the Great War.

The impact of the Great War on Downton has been written about in detail by Edward Green in his excellent book.[5] He recites that approximately two of every nine servicemen from Downton were killed, representing 22% of the those who joined up.[6] To put this figure in perspective, the percentage of deaths per servicemen in the British

Percy Hayter, formerly a grocer's assistant who lived in Slab Lane, and Bert Newman (Margaret Smith).
Both joined up in 1914 and both survived although Bert's brother Fred was killed in 1917 and has no known grave. He is commemorated on the Tyne Cot Memorial in Belgium. The Newmans lived in a cottage now called Cymbeline in The Borough and ran a shop there.

Sergeant William Newman (front centre) in the trenches in 1915 (Margaret Smith).

Empire as a whole was approximately 10%.[7] There were eleven Wiltshire battalions, though not all Downton men served in them but they were prominent in areas of heavy fighting throughout the war. The casualty statistics for Downton servicemen tell their own story.

The first of the forty-four Downton men killed was Private George Henry Hobbs of the First Battalion Hampshire Regiment who died of his wounds on 28th August 1914 aged 19, shortly after the retreat from Mons. The last was Able Seaman Reginald James Nicklen. He died on 22nd September 1919, drowned while taking part in the post-war exercises supporting White Russia against the Bolsheviks, a conflict regarded as part of the Great War because the Bolsheviks were able to seize power in Russia while it was crippled by its conflict with Germany and Austria-Hungary.

As if the casualty figures for Downton men in this conflict were not enough, the village suffered one of the worst floods in its history, in 1915. 125 houses were flooded for two weeks in January and a smaller flood occurred in the following month.[8]

The majority of Downton men served in the army but they also filled positions in the navy, royal army flying corps and royal naval air service. They served in many different regiments. Most joined up as volunteers in1914 though some were already regular servicemen when war broke out, such as Edward Blake, an army sergeant. Downton men saw action in several theatres of war, including Turkey and the Middle East but the majority of those who died were killed on the

Western Front. Of the forty-four who died, twenty have no known grave and four of these, Bob Bundy, Frederick Bennett, George Hobbs and Ernest Smith, died of wounds. Despite being in medical care when they died and were interred, their graves were lost as the front line shifted back and forth across the same ground.

William Charles (Charlie) Weeks lived in a small thatched cottage, now 59 The Borough, and he enlisted as Charles Weeks. His home was a two-up two-down cottage with no electricity, running water or inside toilet, and he lived there until he died long after the war. His makeshift kitchen had a pump for water and his toilet was a bucket in a shed at the bottom of the garden. He was a small, quiet and unassuming man who never married. He served in the army throughout the war but never once spoke of it afterwards. When he died in 1960 his family found his army service medals in a drawer, still in the envelope and box posted to him from the War Office. The box had never been opened, the medals never put on their ribbons, all simply hidden away, a memory not to be recalled.[9]

Winifred Isaacs like most of her generation, never spoke of the war either and four years after the conflict ended she married Ted Isaacs, an ex-soldier from Nunton. Winifred, the daughter of George Futcher, Downton's last hayward, lived in Gravel Close and was a volunteer nurse during the war, although she did not serve abroad. She wrote to many of the soldiers, as did several other Downton girls, to raise their morale. Professional soldier Sergeant Edward James Blake, a Downton man whose family lived at 61 The Borough, regularly sent Winifred photographs and hand-embroidered greetings cards from France until he was killed in 1918 near the Somme battlefield. Blake

The Newman's cottage in The Borough during the flood in 1915 (Margaret Smith).

Charlie Weeks and Winifred Isaacs as a volunteer nurse (Author's collection).

had already received wounds three times previously during fighting, on all occasions returning to active service. The third time, wounded during the battle of the Somme, he was sent back to a hospital in England, with a gunshot wound to the hand and shell shock. In one of his handwritten cards he subsequently sent from France to Winifred he said how much he had enjoyed walking in the meadow with her. The card dated 4th April 1917 reads:

> My dear Win,
> I now take the greatest pleasure in writing these few lines to you, dear, hoping to find you in the pink as it leaves me the same. Well dear, I am sending you a couple of these postcards in a great hurry as we only got them tonight and we are very busy of course I cannot tell you in what way. So dearie I hope you will excuse me. Well love, I have had my photo taken but I cannot say when I shall have the chance to get them as we may be far away from here soon, so, dear Win, I am in hopes that we shall soon be able to have what we have been talking about so long you know. I love those <u>rides</u> and <u>walks</u>, what. Well dear, I will now conclude so with heaps of love and kisses I am yours, xxxxxxxxxxJim.[10]

He died less than a year later when a first aid hut in which he was sheltering was struck by an enemy shell. Winifred never revealed her relationship with Edward, whatever form it may have taken, but she kept his cards and photographs in a drawer in her bedroom, where they were found after she died.[11]

The death toll was huge although the majority of servicemen returned. Nevertheless the war changed them all profoundly and the contrast with the experience of those left at home was often difficult. Particularly tragic was the case of Reginald Durdle, whose parents lived at number 19 High Street. His body was found in the river by Bert Eastman in 1923; the coroners verdict was suicide.[12] For others like Albert Futcher, Winifred's brother, the war brought opportunities. He had joined the Royal Navy shortly before hostilities broke out and was selected during the war for service in the Royal Naval Air Service working on the construction and testing of airships. He learned engineering and radio telegraphy skills and was the first of his family to make a living away from agriculture. He met and later married Katherine or Kitty Austin while he was based in London. To impress her while courting he made her a tiny metal boot hook for unlacing long boots, which he then dropped into her garden in south London from an airship. Only later did he reveal to her a secret compartment in the handle of the boot hook which contained a tiny handwritten love note.

Edward James (Jim) Blake

Edward Blake's grave in Achiet-le Grand cemetery in France (Author's collection).

Thought to be Edward Bonvalot of
Wick House (Margaret Smith).

Charlie Weeks, Edward Blake and Albert Futcher were all working
men from families long associated with agriculture in Downton.[13]
By contrast Edward Bonvalot was an old Etonian and a Cambridge
graduate whose family lived in Wick House. He died of wounds
sustained during a German attack on the Western Front near Arras in
October 1915. The war also claimed the life of Sir Edward Hulse of
Breamore House. The war was a great leveller and privilege brought
no immunity; even Raymond Asquith, the Prime Minister's son,
whom Winston Churchill referred to as 'my brilliant friend', died in
fighting. The Commonwealth War Graves Commission, founded by
Fabian Ware, made no distinction between the rank or class of service
personnel they laid to rest.

The Great War ended on 11th November 1918 and the armistice
brought mixed reactions. There was celebration, relief and a welcome
for returning heroes, tainted with grief for the loss of so many. The
deaths of forty-four men from the village meant that everyone knew
someone who would never return. Life was particularly hard for
widows with children. Sergeant Harry Noble died of pneumonia in
France in February 1916. His widow had to leave their tied cottage,
after which she moved to a cottage on Lode Hill. She worked at the
tan yard, also taking in washing to make ends meet and to support her
three children.[14]

The interwar years brought hardship too, but Downtonians tried
to return to a normal life facilitated by some safeguarding of the

Doctor Whitehead senior with Miss Squarey of Moot House (WI Scrapbook).

emerging welfare state and the improving state education which gave them a better chance of social mobility. Some eighty years previously, Michael Futcher, the young boy caught stealing apples, had given up hope of a better life in England when he emigrated to Canada. His descendant Albert Futcher, born in 1895 and educated in Downton and at Bishop Wordsworth's Grammar School in Salisbury, remained in the United Kingdom and enjoyed a life materially better than his forefathers.

The arrival of Dr. Brian Loder Whitehead in Downton in 1919 also brought benefits to the village. Dr. Whitehead Senior (known as 'Big Brian' at home) was a man of many talents, a Cambridge graduate, a medical graduate from St. Bartholomew Hospital, London, a magician (he performed with his partner Owen Hughes), a war hero (he won a Military Cross for operating under fire during the First World War) and an organiser of many plays and concerts in Downton. His wife

Winifred and three daughters were very keen riders. 'If I'd been a horse I would have been better looked after' was his refrain to his wife.

He bought the Downton practice and Hamilton House in Barford Lane from Dr. Whitely, a former doctor in the village. His granddaughter recalled that he developed a particularly good reputation for delivering babies, and travellers used to come into the area when they were expecting, although in later life he once complained that he was getting too old to crawl around in tents administering to mothers in labour. To his surprise the next time he was asked to attend a birth, the mother was accommodated in a full-sized completely equipped hospital tent, causing Dr. Whitehead to wonder where it had come from.[15]

The war brought profound changes in society, not least in attitudes to women, many of whom had taken over the roles of men away fighting. Changes in fashion, such as the wearing of trousers and shorter skirts and the bobbing of hair were symbolic of a degree of liberation. In 1918 the franchise was awarded to women over thirty years of age and the majority of men over twenty-one. In Downton the first Women's Institute in Wiltshire was formed in 1916.

Initially there was an economic post-war boom as people began to purchase goods they had been unable to buy during the conflict. On the international scene newspapers reported in 1919 that Prime Minister David Lloyd George, President Woodrow Wilson of the USA and President Georges Clemenceau of France had agreed the

Downton girls on a motorbike in the 1920s (Author's collection).

The inauguration of the Downton war memorial outside the Memorial Hall (Margaret Smith).

terms of the Versailles Settlement which formally ended the war. This dictated the fates of Germany, Austria-Hungary and Turkey. Despite some misgivings there was optimism and a sense that the war had been fought for a good cause, to maintain the balance of power in Europe and to suppress aggression. Hopes were pinned on the newly founded international peace keeping body, the League of Nations, to ensure that the recent conflict would be 'the war to end wars'. That at least may have given some comfort to the parents, wives and children of the fallen.

Discussions were held in Downton on how best to commemorate the war dead. It was decided to place a memorial in front of what was then named the Public Hall and which has since been renamed the Memorial Hall. This was the building which had originally been the British School, closed in 1896, and it was subsequently used to stage various public events including plays and films. Following discussions between the trustees of the Hall and the War Memorial Committee it was decided that a memorial, naming every man from Downton who had given his life, was to be placed on the front of this building. A new portico designed by Bernard Masters was commissioned and the stone plaque engraved with the forty-four names of Downton's fallen was attached to the outer facing wall. Alterations to the hall were carried out by a firm of local builders, Downer and Bailey. The war memorial was dedicated on 27th March 1921. A similar memorial had already been unveiled in Downton Baptist Church in May 1920 and another was placed in Downton Parish Church in June of that year. A list of all those who were on active service in the war was also placed on a large wooden plaque inside the Memorial Hall.

Edward Bonvalot's mother, Mrs. Emily Bonvalot, purchased the land adjacent to the Memorial Hall in 1921 to create a garden in memory of her son. She wrote to the Parish Council, stating:

> It is my desire to present to the village, as a memorial to my late son, the small field adjoining the Memorial Hall, to be a public garden, a portion of which might be used as a play ground for children.

The Memorial Garden was officially opened on 5th August 1922 and it has been enjoyed as a place of peace and recreation by generations ever since.

However even before the Downton war memorial had been dedicated, the Paris Peace Settlement of 1919 had been challenged and war broke out between two of the former protagonists, Greece and Turkey. In the years which followed, the prospect of another international conflict loomed. At home the post-war boom faltered and by 1921 unemployment had risen. In these years disillusion about the Great War set in, fanned by the economic downturn as well as by the war poets who had written with passion about its horrors. The interwar years in Downton brought mixed fortunes. The tanning

An early photograph of the Memorial Gardens (Margaret Smith).

industry was booming, so much so that in 1919 the works were extended and a new multi-storey building was added.[16] The paper mill opposite the tannery closed and the Southern Tanning Company purchased its buildings and machinery.

As a postscript to the war the Salisbury Journal reported that when the vicar of Downton, the Revd. Charles Simister, moved into the parish to take up his post in 1960, he found a live German incendiary shell dating from the First World War in the attic of the vicarage. Described by army disposal experts as 'fairly dangerous' no-one knew how it came to be there, but it was presumed that a soldier brought it home as a souvenir.

Across the country there was a decline in agricultural profits, particularly from sheep farming and arable land, both of which had sustained Downton for centuries. A predominant feature of the interwar years was the selling of land by the great estates. High death duties and a rise in labour costs contributed to the trend and the propertied classes were forced to make economies. Locally the Radnor estate sold off a large number of cottages in Downton at this time. They employed fewer staff in their houses and fewer labourers on the land. This closed many employment opportunities though it gave some tenants the chance to become owner occupiers for the first time. Many areas of water meadows began to fall into disuse, although Catherine Meadow in Downton continued to be regularly drowned to provide early grass for cattle until after the Second World War.

There was a significant amount of political unrest in the country as a whole between the wars and Downton did not entirely escape it. In 1919 a demonstration was staged in Downton by the Agricultural Labourers and Rural Workers Union. In the same year the staff at Downton railway station came out on strike in support of a national dispute over pay. Another area of disquiet was the level of government support for ex-servicemen and dependants of war casualties. In Downton, the Comrades of the Great War, an ex-servicemen's association, passed two resolutions in 1919 stating that the demobilisation payment to servicemen and the pensions for wounded ex-servicemen were inadequate. It was a significant grievance in an era when people were unaccustomed to complaining and unwilling to do so. Over six million men had served in the war and of those who came back 1.75 million suffered some kind of disability and half of these were permanently disabled.[17] To this figure could be added those who were dependants; the wives and children, widows and orphans as well as the parents who had lost sons in the war. For Harry Noble's widow, life remained a struggle. The establishment of the Royal British

Legion in 1921 by Tom Lister helped bring charitable support to those who were not being adequately helped by the government.

The interwar period is beyond living memory for all but a few at the time of writing. Fortunately Fred Chalk, who was born in Downton in 1903 and lived in the village in the1920s before joining the navy recalled his early life in a letter.[18] His description speaks for itself:

> At the age of 10 I helped my father on New Court Farm, under the gentleman farmer, Neddy Main. I milked ten cows every morning, starting at 6 a.m. My gift for that was a lovely glass of milk from the cooler. I did various other jobs. Before school I collected the papers from the station, which my mother delivered, cleaned boots and shoes at Fairfield House. After school I collected the evening papers from the station and delivered them on the way home and then at Fairfield House I cleaned the steel knives, chopped wood and filled the coal scuttles. Then for my year working at Middle Wick Farm for H. Butler, on a winter evening I purchased ten rabbits at nine pence each off the shoot and sold them round the village at ten pence, one shilling or one shilling and three pence, depending on size. This was really hard work.[19]

In agriculture there was a trend towards market gardening throughout the south of England and in Downton several fields bordering the Salisbury to Ringwood road were turned over to crops such as lettuce and strawberries. The railway through Downton allowed convenient transport to markets. Further afield, the continued development of large tracts of Salisbury Plain for military training, which had begun in 1897, and the rapid growth of the Port of Southampton provided employment in new areas. In Downton local amenities and services began to improve from the 1920s with the addition of a recreation ground and a new library.

Yet many of the older thatched cottages in Downton were falling into disrepair. The Women's Institute raised the urgent need for more housing with the Parish Council. The first council houses were built in Wick Lane in 1921 and in 1927 electric street lighting came to the village. But one landmark house in the village suffered dramatically in 1923. Moot House caught fire in the night, trapping the maid Gwen Burnham and the cook, Annie Wilson upstairs. In panic the two jumped from a window, but Gwen landed on top of Annie resulting in Annie's tragic death. All remaining members of the staff and the family were saved. It was said at the time that Downton's

Moot House and the Salisbury Fire Brigade after the fire in 1923 (Margaret Smith).

horse drawn fire-engine had just been withdrawn from the village so it took half an hour for the fire brigade to arrive from Salisbury, by which time the house was gutted.[20] Lavinia Carver, a daughter of Mr. Pitt-Squarey, survived the fire but died a few months later.[21] Her children, recognising the shortage of housing in the village, built two semi-detached cottages for those in need, Carver Cottages in Barford Lane, in her memory.

In October 1929 the price of shares on the US stock market plummeted, falling 47% in twenty-six days. The Wall Street crash led to an international economic depression of catastrophic proportions. In Britain the industrial North was most severely affected as companies collapsed and thousands were made redundant. In the South the effects were also apparent but less obvious. The Southern Tanning Company failed but the business was revived in 1935 under the new name of Downton Tanning Company as the economy slowly recovered. A year earlier in 1934 the South Wilts Bacon Curing Company opened a slaughter house and meat processing plant on the site of the old workhouse and the premises for Downton Home Industries at the junction of Green Lane. The business later became Collins Bros and traded under that name until 1970. In 1935 the old grist mill opposite the Tannery reopened as a hydro-electric generating station, operated by Downton Electric Light Company.[22] The Radnor estate was forced again to sell off a number of its Downton properties for financial reasons which meant that many more villagers were able to become owner-occupiers.

In 1935 the village celebrated the silver jubilee of King George V with a street party and a carnival of floats supported by the Downton Band. Unknown to the public the King was suffering from lung cancer and he died on 20th January 1936. He was succeeded by his elder son, David to his family but officially Edward VIII. His accession created a constitutional crisis brought about in part by his marriage to Wallis Simpson. Edward abdicated in the same year in favour of his younger his brother, George VI.

Events in Germany would soon have more serious repercussions in Downton than domestic news. Although the village had largely escaped the worst effects of the Great Depression the economic crash was the most important factor leading to Hitler's accession to power in Germany in 1933. It was in this respect that the Depression had its most profound impact on Downton. When war broke out again in 1939, the village, like every community in the country, was called upon to play its part.

The Downton War Memorial records that in simple numbers the Second World War had a lesser impact on Downton than the First. Service casualties in Britain and the Empire were fewer although there were more civilian casualties. The names of ten from Downton who died for their country are listed, among them a woman, Violet Shelly.[23] She served in the WRAF but was killed in an aircraft accident in

The 1935 Downton Jubilee Pageant (Author's collection).

The Downton War Memorial

Canada in 1944 and is also commemorated on a war memorial in Ottawa.[24]

Particularly tragic is the presence of the names of a father and son among the war dead, Henry and Cecil Phillips. Henry Phillips was serving in the Home Guard when he was killed and he is buried in St. Laurence churchyard in a military grave. He had spent thirty years in the army and the territorials, serving throughout the First World War in Mesopotamia, Palestine, Egypt and Italy. When the Second World War broke out he was the licensee of the Three Horse Shoes public house and too old for active service, but he was one of the first in the area to join the Home Guard. His death at the age of 50 was due to a tragic military training accident at Imber on Salisbury Plain, when a trainee Hurricane pilot mistakenly fired on a group of observers including Henry. There were 81 casualties of which 23 died. The accident occurred on 13th April 1942 during a training exercise in preparation for a visit to the base by Winston Churchill and General Marshall. The visit continued as planned a few days later and Churchill was informed but according to the recent press the incident was covered up for many years. Lt. Phillips is also commemorated on a memorial plaque, unveiled in 2012, in St. Giles Church, Warminster.[25]

The Philips family had moved to Downton between the wars.

Henry's son Cecil was a member of Downton church choir. He left school at fourteen and joined the army boys service. He was later invalided out but, determined to serve his country, he joined the Home Guard for a while before being accepted by the RAF. He was a rear gunner when he was killed over Tunisia.

Each name on the war memorial represents a human tragedy. It is difficult to imagine how families coped with such loss. A notable feature of the names listed for the Second World War is that fewer of the old Downton surnames appear than for the First. People were more likely to move away from their place of birth in the twenty years between the two wars as employment opportunities expanded and so families were less attached to the old communities. Equally many Downton residents have relatives commemorated on memorials all over the country and abroad.

Unknown in Downton at the time but twenty years later the familiar figure in the village, Reverend Charles Simister, was a distinguished war hero. He is remembered as a hard working and dedicated vicar who arrived in the village in 1960 and who cycled around the parish administering to all, not just to his congregation. In the war Corporal Simister was a commando with the RAMC. He took part in Operation Chariot in St. Nazaire in 1943 and was awarded the military medal for his role in the landings at Salerno in the same year. His citation states that he performed his duties.

> ...with complete disregard for his own personal safety, he was responsible for saving the lives of at least six badly wounded men. At Dragone he attended to wounded under direct mortar and machine gun fire from close range and by his actions and coolness of bearing encouraged the members of the troop to remain steady in their positions under heavy fire.

The Second World War is a period within living memory of some Downton residents. A number of servicemen were billeted in Downton, some with local families, others in temporary bivouacs in fields close by. American soldiers took over the stables in Gravel Close (now demolished), the Warren in the High Street, Wick House, fields in South Lane and land beside the Salisbury Road. Downton also received civilian evacuees from Portsmouth, Southampton, Liverpool and London. One evacuee family, the Blakers, were housed in a cottage on the south side of the New Court Carrier. The rivers and meadowland of Downton were both a source of delight but also a danger to newcomers and one small evacuee boy was rescued from drowning by Tony and Phil Perry.[26] Downton children were pleased to have new friends to play with and Margaret Smith recalled that they brought with them different playground games from their own communities.

The Local Defence Volunteers, commonly known as Dad's Army, were formed to defend the area in the event of a German invasion, which was an imminent threat after the fall of France in June 1940. They painted white lines on the road where it crossed the River Avon at Catherine Bridge to indicate where to place a tank trap. Another ploy was to cut branches beside roads and to lay them on the verges ready to drag them in front of enemy tanks. It was thought that a tank driver would stop to clear the debris and while the hatch was open the Home Guard could lob grenades into the tank. An anti-aircraft battery was sited on Barford Down and gun emplacements were sited at strategic points along all railway lines including the Salisbury–Fordingbridge line. Some villagers still remember the string of incendiary bombs dropped along the railway line between Downton station and the tunnel. The importance of this branch line was that it linked to a railway line at Holton Heath near Poole which was a major weapons and ammunition factory and store. For the observant walker there are still visible remains of wartime defence in the area, such as the blockhouse by the railway at Breamore, the remains of a large camp near Ibsley and traces of twelve New Forest airfields. The most important airfield was at Stoney Cross, used as a fighter base until 1944.

The realities of war were vividly highlighted for villagers with the dropping of two land mines very near to houses. One exploded on Catherine Meadow on the east bank of the River Avon. The blast was enormous and the hole it created is still visible as a round depression filled with reeds. The shockwave blew out windows in cottages in The Borough, blew out the doors of the bacon factory and toppled the village cross. The land mine dropped on Barford Down was further away from the village and only caused a cyclist to be thrown from his bicycle. The area was targeted by the German air force because of the presence of airfields in the New Forest.

There was yet more drama when an aircraft, probably a Spitfire, crashed on Lode Hill, near Mitchell's Timber Yard. At least two Downton residents remember seeing the wreckage which was visible from the railway line but the site was quickly cordoned off.[27] During the Battle of Britain in 1940, several villagers witnessed a German aircraft flying over Downton in line with The Borough, but fortunately without any consequences.

The United States entered the war in December 1943 and American troops arriving in Britain early in the following year were billeted in

The Victory Parade in Downton in 1945 (Margaret Smith).

and around Downton. There was a build up of troop numbers towards D Day in June 1944 as Southampton and Portsmouth were two of the departure points for the Normandy invasions. In neighbouring Breamore, the great hall of the House was used by General Patton as his map room in preparation for the D Day landings. He was visited there by King George VI and on one occasion the King, with little advance warning, travelled back from there via Downton station. Despite the confidential nature of the visit, villagers nevertheless managed to deck the station with flags.[28]

A large camp was set up for US and British servicemen and allied forces on the east side of the A338 Salisbury Road, which became known as Tin Town by locals on account of the rows of Nissen huts built to accommodate them. It is now the site of Downton's industrial estate. It was commonplace to see army lorries and tanks parked up or driving through the village. This was for many villagers the first time that Afro-Caribbean people were seen in the village. They suffered racial discrimination and segregation in the southern United States and appreciated the warmth of their local reception and the tolerance and open mindedness of the British people. They returned to the States after the war with a greater determination to campaign for equal civil rights.

The Americans discovered the delights of fishing in the River

The Sherwoods re-united after the war (Pat Cameron).

Avon, but because they used unorthodox and possibly illegal methods stocks soon became depleted until an agreement was reached with the Radnor estate. The river banks were then patrolled by military police as well as the estate's water bailiff. American soldiers, like generations of Downtonians before them, enjoyed swimming and jumping in the river on hot summer days. Sadly one American drowned at Weir Gaps as a result of diving backwards into the river.

There was much socialising in the village between the visitors and locals partly due to American GI Henry Gray, nicknamed HiFi Henry, who organised dances in the Memorial Hall with a collection of dance band records played on a gramophone. These were extremely popular with local girls and with the young servicemen who were far from home and about to risk their lives in the campaign to free Europe from Nazi tyranny. There were a few Downton girls who became GI brides including Vera Philips, the daughter of Henry and sister of Cecil, both of whom lost their lives in the war. Vera later returned home, her second husband being a Downton man.

When Germany surrendered in May 1945 Downton had its own victory celebrations. Villagers marched up Lode Hill in a torchlight procession, carrying sticks wrapped in rags soaked in tar. They lit a huge bonfire surmounted by an effigy of Hitler. One family with less cause to celebrate were the Sherwoods.[29] Harold Sherwood was captured by the Japanese when Rangoon fell in 1942. From March that year after weeks of heavy fighting he was held as a Japanese prisoner of war until the Japanese surrendered in August 1945. Harold suffered terribly at the hands of the Japanese and contracted malaria. The work he was forced to do gave him back problems for the rest of his life and the trauma he suffered had a lasting effect on him. In a photograph he is safely home with his family in 1945, his wife clutching the small handbag he managed to buy for her in Singapore on his return journey. But Harold was a changed man; he never fully recovered and his illness subsequently led to the break-down of his marriage.

At the end of the war the National Government, which was a coalition of all three major political parties, split to fight the General Election. The Conservative party had dominated that coalition and Churchill, its leader, was widely credited as being one of Britain's most effective and popular war-time leaders but his election campaign was a disaster. By 1945 he looked tired and out of touch. The Labour party under Clement Attlee promised to build a new Britain and they captured the spirit of the age with a programme of sweeping peace-time reforms, consequently winning a convincing victory. The Labour government guided by the Beveridge Report of 1942, created a National Health Service which would care for every citizen 'from the cradle to the grave'. The old Victorian attitudes to social welfare were a thing of the past. The creation of the NHS and the Education Act of 1944 which gave free schooling for all children up to the age of 15 affected every man, woman and child for generations to come and built on the foundations laid by the Liberals before the First World War. These were reforms which made a real difference to the lives of all in Downton.

Free access for all to health care was transformational. Dr. Brian Whitehead junior succeeded his father in the Downton practice shortly after the Second World War. The Whitehead family continued to live in Hamilton House with its adjacent surgery. Like his father before him Dr. Whitehead was a much respected general practitioner, although working long hours and answering emergency calls in the middle of the night was the norm for most GPs at that time. With increasing traffic through the village sadly this sometimes entailed being first on the scene at road accidents, particularly at the Catherine Bridge which became an accident black spot. Dr. Whitehead was also called upon to attend farm accidents. He also found time to contribute to village life by helping to organise the annual Downton Carnival and setting up the Eventide Association to give senior citizens an annual outing. His daughter recounts that he was once so busy that he forgot he had visited one exhausted patient, advising bed rest until his return. Two weeks later, horrified, he remembered her and rushed to her house to find her still in bed but looking remarkably fit.[30]

Dennis Musselwhite was a school leaver in the early 1950s. He recalled working on the dairy farm of Mr. Newman at Woodfalls both before and after school to help with the family income and later as a full-time dairyman. Milk was collected by a lorry every morning, in churns each holding about 10-11 gallons. The dairy was lit by paraffin lamps until electricity reached outlying farms in the 1950s. There was some mechanisation of milking, powered by a Lister diesel engine but it was not an easy life.[31]

There was a serious shortage of housing at the end of the war and in Downton the Nissen huts on the Salisbury Road were used as temporary accommodation until new council houses were built in the early 1950s along Moot Lane. The new houses had electricity and running water, facilities which many of the older cottages still lacked. Many residents were pleased to exchange their old cottages for modern amenities. At this time Moot Lane was barely developed and was a quiet single-track lane lined with elm and oak trees. Similarly Gravel Close had just a few cottages along its length. It was at this time in Moot Lane that one of Downton's oldest dwellings was discovered by the occupant of one of the newest houses. In 1953 a council house tenant unearthed the mosaic floor of the Roman villa while digging a hole for his washing line post.[32]

The new housing developments after the war increased Downton's population which had been steadily falling. In 1958 the *Salisbury*

Journal reported in a story featuring the new housing development in Moot Lane that in 1951 there were 1,701 inhabitants against twice that number a century before.[33] The first council houses were in fact built along Wick Lane and still provide family homes. The article went on to suggest that the decline had been due to the loss of local trades and crafts but it was hoped that the arrival of new residents would help to revive the village and the local economy.[34] The Moot Lane estate was followed by the development of the private Wick estate when Wick House School closed in 1964. Both were welcomed by residents in need of more affordable and modern housing.[35]

The hopes expressed in the local press at that time have to a large extent been realised. Although a consequence of development in the village was the damage to parts of historic Downton's centre, particularly with the demolition of several old thatched cottages and their replacement with modern housing and shops; this was often with the encouragement of the local council. The preservation and renovation of character cottages in old Downton required determination and investment in time and money.

In 1956 the bacon factory in the centre of the village employed around one hundred people and former employees attest to the fact that, despite its business as a pig slaughterhouse, the workforce was a happy one. The tannery continued to function until 1998. A small garage on the main road, next to the Bull Hotel gained a national reputation for tuning Minis. Downton Engineering put Downton on every car enthusiast's map.[36] Downton also gained a reputation in the 1960s for its fishing, with keen sportsmen usually staying in the Bull Hotel. It attracted famous figures from the world of show business, including Billy Fury and Eric Morecambe. The development of light industry on the Salisbury road attracted new and varied forms of employment in the second half of the 20th century.

Downton's population continued to grow in the later 20th century which led to the need for a new school, and many cottages were no longer inhabited by farm labourers. Instead families now came from all walks of life with many working adults commuting to Salisbury and Southampton. Although the number of local shops and businesses was very depleted compared to the turn of the century, Downton avoided becoming a dormitory village but rather maintained a vibrant work and social life. It attracted young families and in 1964 a new secondary school was opened, while the old school buildings in Gravel Close became a Church of England Junior School and the former junior school in Barford Lane closed. In its early days the Downton Secondary School struggled to gain a positive reputation because of the Grammar School effect of the Salisbury schools, but renamed

The flood in 2000 -(Env.ironment Agency).

Trafalgar School in 2007 and under new direction it improved steadily.

In 1964 the closure of the Salisbury to West Moors railway line and Downton station was a result of Dr. Beeching's recommendations. Many Downton residents regretted its passing. The last station master was Harry Hepper, who also fulfilled the roles of porter, booking clerk and signalman. On 4th May Harry sold the last ticket to Sue Grice and on that day 100 schoolchildren took the last train to Breamore.[37] This and more has been thoroughly recorded by his two daughters in their excellent account of the life and work of Harry Hepper.[38]

The development of the Downton Industrial Estate from the 1970s has brought significant change to the village. Many companies have come and gone although two have significantly put Downton on the map for different reasons; in 1992 John and Julie Gilbert began brewing in Downton and still produce award winning beers under the Hopback name. In 2007, a Downton couple Bryn and Emma Parry founded Help for Heroes, a charity which aims to support ex-servicemen and women. With its headquarters in Downton, it attracts high profile patrons and to date has raised over £200 million.

In 1980 Peter Waddington, together with his wife Shirley and colleague Chris Pitts revived Downton's ancient Cuckoo Fair. The name had been used since medieval times for spring fairs which coincided with the first call of the cuckoo, but such a fair had not been held since the First World War until its revival in 1980.[39] The fair began as a small country market, with villagers as stallholders accompanied by local musical events and folk dancing. It has grown into one of the largest fairs in the Wessex region and it continues every year, even in inclement weather or with the threat or after-effects of flooding along The Borough.

Our narrative begins and ends with Downton floods. The end of the millennium and the beginning of the new was a difficult time for Downton with a number of serious floods, particularly in December 2000.[40] In August 2002 the Environment Agency announced to a packed meeting in the Memorial Hall that Downton had been given special funding for a flood defence scheme and the plans were unveiled. The Downton flood defences were officially opened in 2004, symbolising a new era for the village.[41] Joan Gwyther who had so calmly described the water filling her sitting room in December 2000 did not live to see the completion of the work but welcomed the plans to benefit the village for generations to come.

Part 2

Tannery employees in the early 1960s:

The back row includes, from left to right, Chris (Tibby) Perry, Fred Shutler, Alan Bryant, Bert Blake, Trevor Green.

Second row from back includes, from left to right, Tom, Ron and Don Moody, Bert Smith, Wilf Sivyour, Doreen Moody, Frank Chalke, Archie Musselwhite, Bernard Bundy.

Third row from back includes, from left to right, Alice Bromley, Claire Griffiths, Stanley Crock, Bernard Miles, Bill Ireland, Charlie Sewell, Don Marks, George Sherwood, Les Bailey, Reg Bailey.

Front row includes, from left to right, Arthur Bishop (with dog), Mr. Grey, Mr. Richardson, Stan Bishop.

(Don Moody).

9

Work

The foundation of Downton owed a great deal to its position at a river crossing in a fertile valley making it a good place to farm and settle. Through much of its early history agriculture was a key aspect of its economy and society. More recently trade and light industry became increasingly important, much of it but not all associated with the river. The aim here is to highlight aspects of working life other than agriculture which have characterised Downton, particularly in recent times, and where possible to trace the history, although space does not allow a complete survey of all types of work undertaken in the village.

Among Downton's oldest residents, Bert Blake[1] remembered that in his youth between the wars there were only three career opportunities for a young man, other than working on the land. These were the Downton Tanning Company in the High Street, Mitchell's Timber Yard on Lode Hill and Hickman Brothers, a grain merchant whose headquarters were in the building later converted into the Granary flats. It was a limited choice of employment but it was probably better than many other rural communities.

Tanning

The tanning of leather from cow hides may be one of the oldest industries in Downton, although the earliest evidence of a tanner in the village is in 1606.[2] In 1710 the tan yard was acquired by Joseph Davis and in the early 1800s father and son, both John Gibbs, were tanners. The *Universal British Directory* of 1791–8 lists a tan yard as one of the principal employers and various trade directories such as Pigot's

Workers at the tannery after the Second World War. Les Ridgley is in the centre of the group (Downton History Group).

and Co. of 1842 and Slater's of 1852, mention tanners so it is safe to assume that production was probably continuous. By 1903 the tanning business was run by Nobes and Hunt Ltd.[3] The Southern Tanning Company took over the site in 1919, constructing the present multi-storey building, but ceased trading in 1930 and the business was then taken over by the Downton Tanning Company which continued trading until 1998.

The tanning site in the middle of the village required a channel to be dug 400 metres upstream carrying water from the River Avon at Weir Gaps.[4] From at least the 13th century the mill stream also powered a fulling mill and in the 18th century a paper mill. At its peak in the early 20th century the tan yard was a major employer of up to seventy people processing 750 hides a week for the production of shoe leather, shoe soles and saddlery. Tanning spawned leather working crafts such as shoemaking which were evident from the 16th century.[5] Just as the tannery survived into the 20th century so did shoemaking. There were four shoemakers in the village in 1907 but none in 1923.

The method of tanning animal skins was handed down almost unchanged for centuries, and the processes and working conditions of the Downton tan yard are within living memory. It began with washing the hides; in early times in Downton this was done in the river. With commercialisation and development came increasing

Inspecting the hides: From left to right; either Bill Ireland or Chris Perry, Joan Swanborough, Tich Carter (Downton History Group).

The tanning pits in 1947, with Archie Musslewhite and Bert Blake in the foreground (Downton History Group).

mechanisation. The skins were then soaked in huge vats of alkaline, either slaked lime, wood ash or urine to speed up the removal of hair and fat. Each day the hides were manually moved to a fresh solution. Then followed the process of de-hairing, in earlier days by workers with knives, later by machine. Following another wash the hides were cut into strips, soaked in a de-liming solution of hydrochloric acid and then hung on frames in the tanning pits to preserve them and soften their texture. In the case of Downton the tannin was once sourced from oak bark and roots, and later a form of mimosa extract, imported from South Africa, was used. The hides were gently rocked to allow even distribution of tannin; the mechanism being driven by a water wheel. Finally the hides were rotated in drums with fish oil to soften them before drying. Systematic rolling and stretching during the drying process ensured the production of smooth and uniform leather. The process of moving the hides through a succession of solutions could take months and was very labour intensive; it was the skill of the tanner to know when to move the hides from one vat to the next.

Tanning was an unpleasant, hazardous and smelly occupation and tanners were often notable for the distinctive odour which clung to their clothes. Tanneries were usually sited away from habitation but in Downton houses, pubs, shops and the church were all close to the tannery in the High Street. River pollution was high in the early days and the pungent smells which wafted across the village were unforgettable. For those who worked in the tan yard there were serious risks to health. Les Ridgeley worked for the Downton Tanning Company for most of his adult life from the age of 14. He recited an alarming absence of simple health and safety precautions, no guard rails around the open tanning vats and unshielded spinning belts which drove the machinery powered by a water wheel and latterly by electricity. The large uncovered vats were separated only by narrow walkways. Bert Blake also worked in the tannery most of his life. His job was to pull hides out of a treatment vat and put them in the next. He remembered that the workers were all paid piecework, according to quantity: 'You didn't work, you didn't get paid.'

Men stood at the edges of the open vats, walking across them on planks and hauling the skins out with large poles. On one occasion Les fell into a vat and narrowly escaped with his life. The work left him with permanent back problems caused by dragging and lifting the hides.

Shortly after the end of the Second World War some men tried to form a union to fight for better working conditions, but they were warned by the management never to set foot inside the tannery again if they continued with their intentions. However they did win one extra day's holiday a year and better protective clothing.[6]

The products became increasingly specialised and included high quality leather for saddles, but with the advent of synthetic materials

Tannery workers processing hides (Downton History Group).

the business declined and finally closed at the end of the 20th century. The front façade of the Downton Tannery still dominates the centre of the village; it was built in 1919 when older industrial buildings were demolished by the Southern Tanning Company and the current building was constructed. Behind it, stretching along the mill stream bank, was an enormous single storey wooden building which housed the chemical vats. This was demolished to make way for the Church Leat housing development. The water wheel which drove the belts remains in place and can still be seen today.

Mills

Opposite the tannery building there stands a complex straddling the mill leats and dating from the 18th and 19th centuries. They are now residential properties but from medieval times they occupied the site of a number of mills which harnessed water power for various purposes. In 1086 Domesday Book recorded that the bishop of Winchester held seven mills in Downton.[7] It is likely that at least three of them were situated on or near the tannery site, making use of the leat dug from Weir Gaps and running east of the main river. It is difficult to date the digging of the leat, which rejoined the river north of Old Court and it was later supplemented by another channel dug east of Old Court, turning that site into an island. These channels and the island of Old Court are still there today.

The earliest evidence for a fulling mill is in 1215 and it appears to have been one of the earliest in Wiltshire. Later there is a reference to

The mill site.

a fulling mill in Downton in the Winchester Pipe Roll of 1301-2; in that year the rent of 10 shillings lapsed because a tenant could not be found.[8] Fulling mills mechanically cleansed and felted woollen cloth by beating it with wooden fulling hammers operated by a cam driven by a water wheel. Downton had a plentiful water supply, wool from sheep on the downs above the village and a woollen market centred in Salisbury. The fulling mill may have had mixed fortunes as it was derelict by 1349 although by the early 16th century it was again leased to a fuller, William Potter. The decline of the woollen trade from the 16th century may have contributed to Downton's failure to grow and urbanise.

When Downton was leased to secular landlords in the 16th century, the mill complex passed as a single property and included by then two corn mills, one of which may have been for malt, and a mill house. By 1845 the complex situated on the downstream side of the present mill bridge, comprised flour, grist and paper mills as well as a tool grinding shed. Profits were supplemented by leasing fishing rights, trapping eels and charging for water taken from the mill leat.

The paper mill at the western end of the mill building complex may have been in operation since the demand for paper increased in the late 15th century following the invention of printing. It produced paper from at least 1710 and the first known papermaker was Samuel Snelgar who had four apprentices by the middle of the century, John and Joseph Snelgar, John Berryman and John Davis. In the last two decades of the century Joseph Jellyman produced paper there and the mill remained in use until the First World War.[9] In the late 19th century it was run by Wiggins, Teape, Carter and Barlow, which company became well-known for the production of high quality writing paper. In the early 20th century it was acquired by Mark Palmer and Sons but ceased trading in 1919. It was converted into an electricity sub-station in 1929.[10]

Electricity

In a publication entitled *Southern Beam*[11] in 1956, there is an account of the Downton generating station which was the Southern Division's smallest electricity generating unit. It was driven by two turbines housed in a position formerly occupied by a water wheel used for grinding corn in the old grist mill.[12] The first of the two turbines was a Brush diesel with an output of 100kW and the second was a water turbine driven by the river flow, of 60kW output. The diesel engine was ordered from the Brush Company in Loughborough, in June 1933. It was an important engine as it was the first ever Brush diesel engine made and was given serial number 150. It was designated a 4S8 type, which means 4 cylinders, horizontally opposed layout, with cylinder sizes of 8½inch bore and 16½inch stroke, developing 120/160 bhp at 290 rpm. It was delivered to Downton in December 1933. On 28th July 1934, Mr F H Campkin, Secretary of the Downton Electric Light Co. Ltd, wrote to Brush with the following comments:

> Dear Sirs,
> With reference to the 4 cylinder 160 HP Diesel Engine you supplied to us last year for our hydro-electric station, you will be pleased to hear that, particularly during the recent drought, the engine has been called upon to run night and day, and on full load for long periods. You will be very interested to know that the engine has run with practically no supervision whatever as we have only one shift engineer and most of his time has been spent on his outside work.

After the Second World War the station was run single handedly by Steve Horner who worked as electrician, turbine driver, switchboard attendant, diesel plant operator, local station superintendent and eel trapper. Perhaps the outside work referred to here was that of eel staging

The building had a closely slatted floor just above the level of the river, where a number of ramps or hatches could be lowered into the water. The river level was raised by opening sluices and lowering hatches, usually at night, into the swiftly flowing water. This operation forced the water through the traps leaving the eels to be collected in the morning. The business of 'eel staging' was permitted by the Avon Catchment Board from mid June until the end of December; the best month was October. Steve Horner reported that the best catches were made on dark moonless nights when a good catch might number 200

Steve Horner with his eel trap. (*Southern Beam Magazine*).

while the record for one night was 740. The catches were packed into water tight boxes and sent by rail from Downton station to London, one condition of acceptance at the Billingsgate fish market in London being that the eels were still alive on their arrival. The *Southern Beam* magazine recalled that:

> The good folk of Stepney, Canning Town and Limehouse are very partial to jellied eels.

In the 1950s the average price for eels was 2s. 9d. per pound (about 13 pence in today's money but worth considerably more at that time). The Downton generating station's accounts for 1955 recited that the running expenses of the station including wages, diesel oil and maintenance was £37 for the September quarter when the revenue from the sale of eels alone was £43 in the same period.

The generating station closed in 1973. Steve Horner continued to live on the premises and was remembered by many in the village as a talented wood carver in retirement. When several trees fell in the Moot in the great storm of 1987, Steve carved ornaments from the timber, donating proceeds to the Moot Trust.

Lace

While tanning and milling were largely male occupations, many women of the parish from at least the 16th century were involved in the cottage industry of lacemaking. Local tradition suggested that this craft was brought to the area by Huguenots fleeing religious persecution in Europe but this cannot be verified. In 1700 a Salisbury lace dealer reported there were lacemakers in Downton.[13] The *Universal British Directory* of 1791-98 stated in the entry for Downton that 'the principal occupation of the poor is lacemaking'. Its importance in the local economy is attested by the fact that in 1752 the parish paid for two lace-making apprentices. Several lace-making schools were set up in the village, which taught the craft to children aged five and upwards. They survived into the 19th century. Although the schools kept this ancient craft alive, their teaching and working practices would be classed by today's standards as child labour. In those times their meagre wages might have been important for their families.

There are many hundreds of different Downton lace patterns and all have names, such as Downton Daisy and Egg and Rasher. Downton lace was made on a type of pillow tightly packed with straw on which the lacemaker pricked out the design with pins and then worked the cotton threads around the pins using wooden bobbins. Some of these bobbins were decorated with incised lines filled with wax to depict birds and flowers. The oldest bobbin in existence is in Salisbury Museum and dates from 1789.[14]

Lacemaking provided an important income supplement for working families in Downton but despite government attempts to protect the home industry, lacemaking struggled against the competition from machine manufactured lace during the industrial revolution. In 1852 Slater's Trade Directory reported that lacemaking had been important in Downton but this was no longer the case. Hand lacemaking all but died out in the 20th century but in Downton it survived, thanks to the efforts of two local ladies. Mrs. Plumptre and Mrs. Robinson founded Downton Home Industries under the patronage of the Countess of Radnor and collected together more than 500 lacemaking patterns in the early part of the 20th century. Nevertheless when Bertha Kemp wrote an article on Downton lacemaking for the WI scrapbook in 1956 she believed she was the only person in the village still making lace at that time.[15]

But the craft survived and in April 1960 Downton Lace Industries, a volunteer group of 30 lacemakers, presented six lace - edged handkerchiefs to HRH Princess Margaret on the occasion of her marriage to Antony Armstrong-Jones. Downton lace was also presented to HRH Princess Anne when she married Captain Mark Phillips in 1973. In 1981 Diana, Princess of Wales wore Downton lace at her wedding and Downton Cuckoo Fair Princesses continue to be crowned with Downton lace every year.

Basket Making

The craft of basket-making has existed for many centuries in Downton. The evidence for exactly when it began is unclear but there was a family of basket-makers called Rhodes or Roads in the 17th and 18th centuries.[16] An early trade directory of 1793 lists Samuel Eastman as a basket-maker[17] and the Women's Institute Scrapbook claims the foundation of a basket workshop in 1801 in Poplar Cottage by Henry Eastman. By the mid 19th century his son, also Henry, expanded the business to include furniture, cradles and bird cages using withies or willow twigs cut locally. Later the withies were obtained from other sources. Eastman workmanship gained a reputation well beyond the local area and in the Second World War Eastman wicker hampers were dropped by parachute over enemy occupied Europe. A second workshop was opened in the Eastman family home, which comprised a row of three cottages adjacent to Catherine Bridge.[18] The cottage nearest the river was turned into the basket workshop, which extended full height into the apex of the roof. It was next to steps into the river where Gilbert Eastman soaked the withies. The steps are now gone,

Downton's basket works.

considered too dangerous by planners when the flood defence wall was built in 2002, although they had been used without any recorded mishap as a favourite bathing station and fishing spot for local people.

A branch of the Eastman family emigrated to America when in 1638 Roger Eastman sailed to the USA on the *Confidence*. George Eastman of Eastman-Kodak fame was born in 1854 and was a direct descendant of Roger Eastman. Another member of the family, Thomas

Gilbert Eastman at work (Eastman family website – Carol Nelson).

Eastman, emigrated to South America in 1813, leading to branches settling in Argentina, Chile, Uruguay and Ecuador, and there are still local descendants living in and around Downton.[19]

Green Lane

At the junction of Green Lane and The Borough are two tall whitewashed buildings, now converted to residential use. In former times they housed a variety of small industries. Nearer The Borough, the building now known as The Granary was once the premises of Hickman Brothers, grain merchants and millers. Brothers Ernest and Garnet Hickman bought the business in 1922 from Billy Harding and the business of J. Read forage merchants, taking over the lorries and keeping the drivers. Garnet sold his share of the business in 1931 to Ronald and Jack, the two sons of Ernest Hickman and his wife Alice. Ronald and his wife Kathleen lived in the house alongside the mill and often complained that the mill engine caused the whole house to shudder. They produced feed for pigs and poultry. In 1946 the Hickmans sold the business to the grain merchants, Christopher Hill, although the name of Hickman Brothers was kept until 1964, when the building was sold eventually to John Critchley, an entrepreneur who specialised in buying and selling bankrupt stock for the building trade, trading as Critchcraft. The building was converted to residential use in 1990.

The other three-storey building with a gable was built in about 1730 as a workhouse and gaol, and a smallpox isolation hospital was adjacent. The workhouse was set up by the parish in 1731 as a result of Knatchbull's Act[20] and was administered by four parish overseers elected annually. They were obliged to account for all their expenses

The site of the workhouse and the bacon factory.

The site of the granary.

in providing poor relief and the records make interesting reading. For example in 1786 a Mr. Fanstone was paid slightly over £24 for weeding The Borough (presumably a year's wage) and in the same year a nurse was paid 18 shillings for attending to smallpox victims. In 1804 the workhouse was still running and it housed 32 men and 60 women,[21] a shocking figure by todays standards of care and density of accommodation. By 1837 it was empty, because by this time the Poor Law was administered from Alderbury. Between 1904 and 1927 there was a carpet factory behind this building, established by Wilton Carpets. At various times in the 20th century the large upper rooms of the workhouse building were used as a Unionist Club and a meeting

Bacon factory workers (Downton History Group).

room for the Women's Institute, before conversion to industrial and business premises.

In 1929 the South Wilts Bacon Curing Company converted the workhouse building, which still housed cells at the back, into a slaughterhouse and bacon curing factory. However the company soon faced financial difficulties and it was taken over by I. Beer in 1934, a meat distribution company. I. Beer refurbished the workhouse premises and built new industrial units at the rear. At its largest capacity in the 1950s and 1960s it employed about one hundred people and slaughtered 16,000 pigs a week.[22] The factory site was extensive, occupying a prime central position in the village, and was easily identified by its tall brick chimney at the back and large iron gates across what is now Green Lane. Despite the inherently unpleasant nature of the work, several former employees recalled it as a cheerful and comradely workplace. Live pigs were brought in, humanely slaughtered and their meat was processed into sausages, pies, faggots, bacon and gammons. Fertiliser, bone meal and glue were by-products. Among its perks was the proximity of some excellent fishing positions for workers in their lunch hours, as part of the factory site was adjacent to the River Avon just south of Catherine Bridge. Local residents remembered meaty smells wafting over the neighbourhood, a worryingly large population of rats in nearby watercourses and at least one escaped pig. The factory closed in 1968 and became the premises for the Chemical Pipe and Vessel Company, whose owner also purchased the triangular parcel of land on the opposite bank of the river in order to build a house for his retirement. The house, 116 The Borough, was built but the owner predeceased its completion. In the 1990s the factory site was purchased by a developer, who re-instated Green Lane as a public road

Downton Engineering in the early days (Mark Foster).

Daniel Richmond
(Mark Foster,
Mark1 Performance
Conversions).

and built the residential properties along its length. The riverbank area was designated a public space, thus preserving the fishing tradition, not just for factory employees but for all. It is also the site of the Environment Agency flood defence pumping station and a plaque to commemorate the opening of the flood defence scheme.

Downton Engineering

In 1947, while Britain was still subject to post-war rationing, a small garage close to the Bull Hotel on the Headlands was taken over by Daniel and Bunty Richmond. The site in Downton was reputedly chosen because Daniel was a very keen fisherman. The couple built up a good reputation from the servicing, repair and tuning of vintage motor cars. In the mid 1950s a customer asked Daniel Richmond to fit a tuning kit to a Morris Minor. Daniel was dissatisfied with the proprietory kit as it made the A series engine noisy and difficult to drive and so he told his customer that he, Daniel, could do better himself.

Daniel and his team started producing performance tuning kits for

The Bull Hotel with the site of Downton Engineering to the left in the 1950s (Margaret Smith).

most of the widely available cars of the day. For reasons long forgotten the garage began to specialise in BMC A Series engines, fitted to a large proportion of cars on the road at the time.

The couple were somewhat eccentric but Daniel was a gifted engineer. He worked hard and spent his spare time competing in hill climbs and time trials in a variety of modified cars. Bunty Richmond also raced and was regarded as a formidable lady who was not to be crossed by the employees, her customers or by Daniel himself.

In December 1961 the magazine *Autocar* published a very complimentary review of a Downton Engineering converted Mini Cooper that had achieved 100mph and was quieter and more economical than the factory produced model. When news of this conversion kit reached the management of the British Motor Corporation, Daniel was invited to demonstrate the performance of his tuning kits and his expertise to them, resulting in Downton supplying modified engine components for BMC's Competition Department race and rally cars. Daniel was offered and given a design consultancy role with the company, drawing on his particular expertise in engine cylinder head modifications.

As the business grew the premises moved to just north of Long Close on the main road. Downton Engineering was renowned for its high standard of work and dedicated body of employees who were encouraged to fit modification parts to their own cars as part of the company's research and development. The company undoubtedly benefited from the image of the Mini as a symbol of the Swinging Sixties, a classless car favoured by pop stars and royalty alike. Downton's quality of workmanship and success in racing and rallying, including the Monte Carlo Rally, were key factors in the growth of the company. Downton tuned Minis could achieve up to 23mph more than a standard Mini Cooper and clients included the designer of the Mini, Alec Issigonis, as well as Enzo Ferrari and the film star Steve McQueen. In the heady days of the late 1960s Downton Engineering was the most celebrated employer in the village. The firm went into decline with the premature death of Daniel Richmond in 1974 and folded shortly after the death of Bunty a year later.

The Saw Mill

When Bert Blake reminisced about the employment opportunities in Downton between the wars, Mitchell's Saw Mill had already been established for a century. It was situated on Lode Hill where the most recent premises were built in 1925 and they were the headquarters for the company's eight other centres. Wood was imported from abroad and came from their own estates in the New Forest, where the company also supported the dying craft of hurdle-making. Mitchells also owned the brickworks in Moot Lane. With timber and bricks to hand locally, Downton builders and craftsmen did not have far to travel for materials. The local builders, Downer and Bailey merited a special mention in the WI Scrapbook for the quality of their workmanship in the 1950s. Fred Bailey born in 1866 originally came to Downton in the 1890s to help his brother, a builder and blacksmith. Their father was a carpenter and one of his mainstay occupations was making paupers' coffins out of four rough elm boards, with holes each end to insert a rope. As an old man in Downton Fred remembered holding the candle by which his father worked when daylight faded. Times have changed and sometimes for the better.

Reproduction of the 1855 Ordnance Survey map of Downton.(Crown copyright).

10

Road & Rail

Before the building of bridges, fording the river at its shallower points or crossing by boat were the only two options. Nowadays Catherine Bridge crosses the main river, with three segmental arches and stone cutwaters and a distinctive cast iron balustrade, which presumably gave it the more recent name of the Iron Bridge. An inscription on the south side designates it as a County Bridge. In other words it was an important bridge, its maintenance being the responsibility of the county not the parish and it is dated 1820. The architect was J. Peniston, a distinguished county surveyor and also commander of the Salisbury troop of the Wiltshire Yeomanry, in which capacity he was involved in the suppression of the Swing Riots.[1]

The County Bridge replaced at least one earlier bridge connecting the old village with the new borough. The previous fording point was almost certainly just downstream of this bridge and connected the High Street with Green Lane. This fact is corroborated in memories recorded by the WI in 1956[2] and by Albert Futcher, a riparian owner at River Cottage who was born in 1896. He remembered the river running much clearer and shallower than it does today, and when fishing as a boy he saw traces of a deliberately laid flint walkway in the river bed. Later he would often find quantities of oyster shells and clay pipes in his garden which stretched downriver to the supposed ford, suggesting traffic across the river to and from the end of Green Lane. A graphite sketch by John Constable made in 1820 of the River Avon and St. Laurence church in the background also shows the river at this point to have been broader and shallower.[3] The sketch shows a horse wading in the middle of the river, which would not be possible

Catherine Bridge or Iron Bridge.

today. Although art is not necessarily an accurate representation, in this case the sketch corresponds with memory. The cottages along Green Lane were destroyed to make way for the Bacon Factory in the 1920s and the road was reinstated when these industrial buildings were demolished and a housing development was built in the 1990s.

The majority of ancient trackways and roads ran on an East - West axis, as does Downton's main thoroughfare; the amount of North-South traffic using waterways such as as the Avon goes unrecorded. Ancient trackways tended to follow ridges and hills, which were less likely to be rendered impassable by mud, and descended into valleys only to cross rivers and streams. The possible route of the Anglo

Saxon invaders from near Southampton, across the plateau later to become the New Forest from Cloven Hill and down to the Avon at Hatchett Green, has been discussed in a previous chapter.[4] The river may well have been particularly broad and shallow at Charford, hence the likelihood of a battle there in the early 6th century to defend a crossing. The names of Britford and Longford are also a strong indication that further upstream there were other fordable points.

When Downton became a manor of the bishop of Winchester's estate, in the 8th century, access to Downton from the east probably improved. The most likely route from Winchester to Downton would have been to Pepperbox Hill and then down to Templeman's Farm and into the village via a lane now known as Doctor's Alley. This can be clearly seen on an early Ordnance Survey map of 1855. This route is slightly north of the present road at Lode Hill, which was a later cutting into the hillside made to ease the work of horses pulling carts and wagons towards the forest plateau from the valley.

Before 1206 The Borough did not exist. Doctor's Alley emerges into Barford Lane and its most likely continuation into the medieval village, so far as it can be seen today, is via Snail's Creep which passes directly beside the parish church and comes out in the old centre of the village. As it continues westward, the course of this ancient road is then something of a mystery, bearing in mind the time prior to the creation of The Borough. One route may have wound south to join the ancient ford in Green Lane, but given the siting of Wick Lane, it is likely that another early route wound slightly to the north of The Borough. Long Close could have been a section of this route, which probably lay behind the back gardens of the cottages along the north side of The Borough.

When Peter des Roches laid out The Borough in 1208-9, the site now marked by the village cross, outside the White Horse Inn, became the new crossroads and essentially the new centre of the village. Almost certainly an inn would have been here from very early times. The north-south road from Fordingbridge to Salisbury, before the construction of the present A338 in the 17th century, was Gravel Close and South Lane. The village cross may date from the foundation of the Borough, though it is listed by English Heritage as dating from the 14th century.[5]

In 1285 the Statute of Winchester established the principle that manors and manorial landowners were responsible for the maintenance of roads and tracks, including the obligation to clear edges of cover, to prevent or limit intervention by highwaymen. Present day walkers may enjoy the current hedgerows but should imagine these tracks as open and without the hedges and cover that they invariably have now.

Horse and carriage in the Borough (Don Moody).

Parishes took over responsibility for road maintenance in the 16th century, and this was later supplemented by turnpike trusts in the 18th and 19th centuries, which charged tolls on certain roads. The main Fordingbridge to Salisbury road never was a toll road although the road to Cadnam was one.

Ogilby's road book of 1675 shows Downton's Borough and High Street clearly situated at the crossing point of the River Avon on a road which appears to have branched off at Basingstoke from the London to Devon and Cornwall road. The road to Downton then continued through Hampshire and Dorset to Weymouth. It is a simplistic and not entirely accurate road map but it was used for something like 100 years and would have been influential in directing travellers through Downton, thus literally putting Downton on the map.

From the early 18th century the road to Salisbury following the Avon valley was gradually improved. There had been a thoroughfare on this route since at least the building of Longford Castle in the late 16th century and there may well have been an inn on the site of the Bull Hotel on the Salisbury road since then, although the present building dates from the early 18th century. The Bull was both watering hole and coaching inn and in the 19th century it advertised the provision of a daily coach service to Salisbury.

As coaching later gave way to rail and improved road transport, the

Bull was able to establish a reputation of a different kind. Between the 1920s and the 1940s it developed as a fishing hotel, particularly under its licensee ex-Flight Lieutenant L. Parker after the Second World War. Its name may well have derived from a male fish rather than a bovine male.

Downton's roads and lanes all had local names, some a little strange. Their derivations are mostly forgotten. Slab Lane may come from the old English word slap, meaning slippery. Lode Hill is mentioned above. One can only guess where names such as Snail's Creep, the footpath beside the church, and Jiggy Joggy, the lane from Newcourt towards Charlton, came from. It would be a pity if such local names were ever lost.

The Railway

By 1860 there were two major railway lines in the south of England. The Southampton and Dorchester Railway opened in 1847 becoming the London and South Western Railway in 1848 and there was a direct line from Salisbury to London which began operating in 1854 extending to Exeter in 1860. There followed a need to link these two east-west London and South Western railway lines with a north-south connection. A meeting chaired by the 7th earl of Shaftesbury was held in Salisbury on 20th October 1860 to discuss a proposal, resulting in a motion being unanimously passed stating:

> that in the opinion of this meeting it is desirable that a railway should be constructed to connect Salisbury with Wimborne, Poole and the northern parts of Dorset, and that the line now submitted, traversing the valley of the Avon, near Downton and Fordingbridge, and uniting with the [London and] South Western [Railway] on the east side of Wimborne, is satisfactory for the above purpose

The proposal took the route from Alderbury to the south-east of Salisbury on the Southampton line, through Downton and Fordingbridge, to West Moors, located to the East of Wimborne. Financial problems prevented other proposed extensions and when the Salisbury, Poole & Dorset Junction Railway Bill received Royal Assent on 16th July 1860 only the Alderbury-West Moors section was approved. The new line saved approximately 25 miles in the journey from Poole to Salisbury.

The earth was first cut using a silver spade by the Countess Nelson on 3rd February 1863 in a field two miles north of Downton and close to Trafalgar House, the home of the Earl and Countess Nelson.

Mr. Summers, porter at Downton Station in the 19th century. (W.I. Scrapbook).

The Pile Bridge (Margaret Smith).

The Downton railway tunnel, cut through the chalk between Downton and Standlynch (author's collection)..

The line which became known as the Salisbury and Dorset Junction Railway included a tunnel nearly 100 metres long, officially opened on 20th December 1866, and a pile bridge crossing the river Avon downstream of the Moot. From the beginning the line was operated by the LSWR under an agreement which gave the Salisbury and Dorset Railway Company 55% of the gross receipts.[6]

On 3rd June 1884 disaster struck when the 4.50 train from Downton to Fordingbridge was derailed just south of the pile bridge. Five passengers were killed, two by drowning as some of the coaches plunged into the river. Forty were injured, some seriously. Staff and

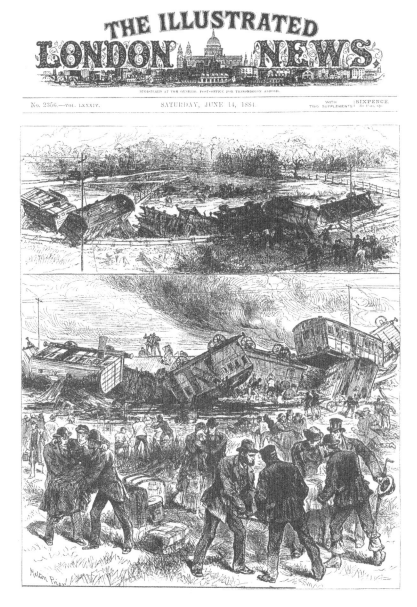

The front cover of the *Illustrated London News*, June 14th 1884, with its depiction of the Downton Rail Disaster.

students of Professor Wrightson's Downton Agricultural College at South Charford Manor rushed to help as did Wrightson and one of his sons. The crash was so serious that it made the front cover of the

Illustrated London News. The exact causes of the crash were fiercely contested but it was subsequently found that the accident was caused by a combination of excessive speed and poor track maintenance. Rail workers blamed both on the railway company and it was particularly noted that staff were frequently under enormous pressure to be punctual.

Downton Station was located to the north of the eastern end of the High Street, the line crossing the road by way of Lode Hill Bridge. The station consisted of a passing loop with up and down platforms plus goods sidings. A steel girder footbridge was installed in 1902; this was the first of its type on the LSWR.

The line was as well-used as any small branch line, serving commuters and school children from Downton, taking day-trippers on journeys to the seaside and bringing audiences to see plays and pageants which were staged in the Moot. It was also a busy goods line; a coal merchant, Clarke and Lush. worked out of the station in the 1950s and 60s and animal skins were transported on the line, destined for the tannery.

Downton's last station master was Harry Hepper.[7] Harry was dedicated to the railway and the village. By the time he retired he was the only employee of the rail company in Downton, acting as station master, ticket clerk and porter. Aside from his normal duties he also released homing pigeons which pigeon fanciers sent in crates on the train to Downton. In 1963, Dr. Richard Beeching, Chairman of British Railways, published his famous report *Reshaping British Railways* which recommended closure of many unprofitable branch

Downton Station at the turn of the century, from a postcard (Margaret Smith).

lines throughout the country. The line through Downton fell victim to Dr. Beeching's axe in 1964 and it was pulled up and all the buildings, except the Station Master's house, were demolished. The name of the road The Sidings is one of the few remaining indications that a line existed and in a controversial planning decision modern houses and bungalows were later built on the line, both in Moot Lane and Hamilton Park. In the Salisbury direction, the tunnel, bridges, cuttings and embankments can still be seen, although most are inaccessible and to the south traces of the line are visible from Moot Lane towards the site of the pile bridge across the Avon, where many a Downton boy used to climb illegally in order to jump into the cool waters in the summer. It is possible to walk part of the line at Burgate and to see the preserved station at Breamore, now a private house.

The loss of the bridge and the failure to use the route as a modern

The last bus passes under the railway arch on Lode Hill before demolition (author's collection)..

Last passengers on the train from Downton; from left to right Gordon Lydford, his wife Freda, Connie and Stan Bishop (Margaret Smith).

day cycle path from Salisbury to Fordingbridge is something of regret for many local people.

By the mid-1970s, Downton was troubled by increasing heavy goods traffic through the village and the threat of unsuitable housing developments on the main Salisbury road which, it was feared, would have led to a further increase in traffic and a strain on local services. The Downton Society was founded in 1975 to protect the village and monitor such planning applications. It successfully fought the application for a large increase in houses to the West of the A338 and was also instrumental in the imposition of a ban on heavy lorries through The Borough and High Street. Their work continues today.

An entrant in the fancy dress competition in the 1963 carnival (Downton History Group – Hill Collection).

11

Prayers & Players

Prayers

Catholic and Protestant

Domesday Book records a church in Downton in 1086, describing it as the church of the manor of Downton with four hides of land. It probably had the status of a minster church and locally would also have served the Saxon communities of Charlton, Wick, Witherington, Walton (New Court), Standlynch and Barford as well as villages further afield. Despite an absence of earlier records a church almost certainly existed from at least the 8th century when the manor was presented to the bishopric of Winchester.[1] It is possible that the bishop appointed a rector from that time. A parson is first mentioned in 1147 and it can be assumed the appointment was made by the bishop of Winchester. The first mention that the bishop of Winchester had the right to appoint the rector of Downton is in 1281 when the king made the appointment because the bishop's seat was vacant in that year.[2]

Downton seems to have attracted a number of distinguished rectors, including Thomas de Charlton in 1318 who became the bishop of Hereford in 1327. Most rectors were non-resident and employed a curate to perform their parish duties. An example is William Burnell who was presented to the Downton living in 1282. The nephew of Edward I's chancellor, Robert Burnell, he was only 21 when appointed. He was not ordained and was given dispensation to live away from Downton to study, by his uncle, the bishop of Bath and Wells. The dispensation was ruled to be contrary to canon law in 1295 and the bishop of Winchester then presented Downton to his clerk, Robert

St. Laurence Church.

of Maidstone. Burnell disputed the appointment until it was finally settled on Maidstone in 1303. It is difficult to imagine that either Maidstone or Burnell had much time to minister to the parishioners of Downton during that time.

A rector had the right to receive tithes, a form of taxation in kind levied by the church, but in 1382 the bishop of Winchester, William Wykeham, appropriated the tithes from Downton rectory to himself to support his foundation of Winchester College.[3] In 1383 he appointed Nicolas de Alresford as Downton's first vicar, a position which excluded the incumbent from his right to receive the great tithes. In 1385 he passed the advowson (the right to appoint) of Downton to Winchester College. The vicar of Downton was only entitled to receive a small portion of the tithes of the parish. A new vicarage was built next to the church on land taken from the rectory garden. A later vicarage was built on the same site in the 17th century and the greater part of the present building, known as Chalkhill House, was built in 1783 by Downton's longest serving vicar, Thomas Lear. There is a memorial in the church to Lear which describes him as a 'beloved vicar of this parish'.

The large parish of Downton required considerable effort to fulfil duties of care properly, and after the bulk of its tithes were given to Winchester College in 1385, vicars complained that the living proved insufficient for them to administer Downton and its attached chapels adequately. Although it was worth 17s. 10d. per annum, comparing favourably with other parish livings, the vicar of Downton had to cover a wide area and almost always employed a curate from his own income. The complaint against Winchester was long lasting, so much so that from 1420 newly appointed vicars had to declare that they were willing to accept in advance such a settlement.

The church of St Laurence is a magnificent cruciform building of flint and brick. It has undergone many alterations, the main ones listed here.[4] The oldest part, the three western bays of the nave, date from the late 12th century and may represent the full extent of the early church. When bishop of Winchester, Peter des Roches, laid out The Borough to create the new market town of Downton in the early 13th century the church was enlarged with the addition of two eastern bays, a central tower, transepts and finally an enlarged chancel which was added in about 1350. The chancel was screened off from the nave and may have served as the bishop's private chapel. The improvements were high quality work and were completed to accommodate a growing population of freeholders attracted by the establishment of the new market town. About a hundred years later the transepts and chancel were heightened and in the 15th century a west door was added. Work inside may have been completed on the nave windows but much was obscured by 17th century work. During the Reformation (discussed in chapter 5) a medieval wall painting, possibly of the Biblical story of the flight from Egypt, was painted over and the rood screen was removed. In 1791 the tower was raised by the earl of Radnor so that he could see it from Longford Castle. It was lowered again in 1859 when the tower was in danger of collapse

The Church of the Good Shepherd and Our Blessed Lady Queen of Angels.

due to its excessive weight, and so it was returned to its former height, although the pinnacles and ramparts from the earlier embellishment were retained.

The church remained within the control of the Roman Catholic faith until Henry VIII's struggle to annul his first marriage to Catherine of Aragon resulted in a formal break from Roman papal authority in 1534. Within a few years all religious communities, including the monastery at Breamore and the abbey at Wilton, were dissolved by royal decree and their buildings and land sold off to royal favourites. It is interesting to note that there were no protests at this action in the Wessex area, as there were further north, suggesting that these religious houses had already lost all public support. Perhaps they were no longer functioning in a way which benefited the local community. Or was the streak of non-conformity and rebellion which appears later in South Wiltshire already apparent in the sixteenth century? If so few tears were shed for the destruction of these traditional religious establishments.

Before the Victorian age Church music was more often than not supplied in the Wessex area by village musicians, playing a variety of instruments. It seems however that in Victorian times the church authorities, influenced by Evangelical movements, increasingly frowned upon the genre of musical accompaniment thus produced. It was all just a little too raucous and enjoyable and was deemed unseemly. Consequently the Church of England sought to install organs in many churches in Wessex, which often led to disagreements with the village musicians.[5] A dispute of this kind is described by Thomas Hardy in his novel *Under the Greenwood Tree* and is almost certainly based on fact, as Hardy's father and grandfather had both been church musicians. The church authorities won in all cases and as a result we see organs being installed in a large number of churches in Wessex in the latter part of the 19th century. Downton's church organ by Sweetland of Bath was installed in 1870, a fine organ indeed, but an instrument which may possibly have cut short or discouraged the teaching and practice of amateur village musicians. It may not be a coincidence that it was shortly after the installation of the organ that amateur music-making in the form of brass bands began to develop in Downton.

When the parish church of St Laurence adopted Protestant doctrines in the 1540s, those Catholics who refused to accept the changes were excluded not just from St. Laurence church. Catholics found themselves on the fringes of society. Between the Reformation and Catholic emancipation in the Catholic Relief Act of 1829, Catholics in Downton had to worship in secretive and miserable conditions. Catholic recusants, as they were known, refused to attend the Anglican Church as required by law and continued to be regarded with a mixture of suspicion and pity.[6] Some may have attended secret Catholic masses which were held at the home of the Webb family at Odstock Manor or later in the 18th century at the home of Mrs. Arundell in Salisbury Cathedral Close. Only in 1846 were Catholics in the area able to worship in a beautiful purpose built church again. This was at St. Osmund's in Exeter Street, Salisbury, designed by Pugin, who, as a recent Catholic convert had been shocked, when he visited Salisbury, at the shabbiness of a small Catholic chapel in St Martin's Lane. Catholics dedicated their new church to St. Osmund and sited it just outside the cathedral close, and in doing so were pointedly reclaiming their saint who is buried within the cathedral's consecrated ground.

In 1914 the 4th earl Nelson dedicated Standlynch Church, which at that time was part of the Trafalgar estate, to the Catholic faith as a tribute to his mother who converted to Catholicism. It was given the title of the Church of Mary Queen of Heaven and St Michael and All Angels. The Nelson family continued to support the Catholic faith by their donation of land in Barford Lane on which to build a small house for a Catholic priest. In 1947, when the Nelson family put Trafalgar up for sale, following demands for death duties and the cancellation of the Nelson pension, they feared the chapel would be deconsecrated and so they donated land on the edge of Downton for the building of a new Catholic Church. This is the site of the present Catholic Church in Downton, the Church of the Good Shepherd and Our Blessed Lady Queen of Angels. Built in 1950, it was intended as a temporary structure to be replaced with a permanent church, but this plan has never materialised.

Non-Conformism[7]

In 1670 the bishop of Salisbury complained of the number of non-conformists in Wiltshire and of 'divers, great and outrageous meetings'.[8] This concern reflects the inescapable fact that non-conformism was very strong in the area, particularly among the lower classes, the evidence being the number of registered places of worship. Research suggests that non-conformism appealed to freeholders and those independent of employers, such as shopkeepers, and it also seems to have thrived in more open communities of several distinct settlements, such as Downton, rather than in small, clustered villages.[9] We can also perhaps trace the strong attraction to non-conformism in the early 17th century to the appointment of a puritan minister, Peter Thatcher, to St. Edmund's church in Salisbury, much against the wishes of the incumbent bishop. Accounts vary but it seems that at

Downton Methodist Church.

a church meeting the removal of a damaged stained glass window in St Edmund's Church was sanctioned. After some delay, Salisbury's MP, Henry Sherfield, who was a radical and a leading Puritan, grew impatient. He attacked it with a pikestaff. He broke not only the window but also the pikestaff and he fell to the floor, apparently injured, where he lay 'a quarter of an hour, groaning'.[10] He was fined £500 in the Star Chamber Court but never paid the fine before he died. His action and subsequent harsh punishment suggests that there was a religious and political battle going on for control of hearts and minds in the district.

Sherfield represented a widely held frustration that there were many vestiges in churches of a pre-Reformation, Catholic era which Puritans such as he abhorred. Puritanism had flowered in the age of the Protectorate, when Oliver Cromwell ruled as Lord Protector, but despite the restoration of the monarchy in 1660 non-conformism continued to wield a considerable influence in South Wiltshire. This is shown by the fact that an early Baptist church was formed near Porton and by 1719 the Baptists had their own chapel in Salisbury.

It may be that when John Wesley came to preach in Salisbury in the middle of the 18th century he found a fertile audience, receptive to his ideas and criticisms of the Anglican Church. His followers built a Methodist chapel in St. Edmund's Church Street in Salisbury and by 1800 there were thirteen Methodist chapels in Wiltshire. The Downton Methodist chapel in the High Street, built in 1896, replaces an earlier Methodist chapel in the village on a different site, the former Cottage Hospital on the corner of Lode Hill and Slab Lane. It was more recently Refells the Butchers and is now two flats. In 1849

Downton Baptist Church.

a group of Methodists broke away for their own doctrinal reasons and formed the Downton Reform Church. They met originally in a building now marked by the site of Chapel Cottage, near Tannery House. The chapel on Lode Hill continued in use until it closed in 1919. This group later met in a cottage until the headmaster of the British School let them use two cottages he owned in the High Street. It was on this site that the present Methodist Chapel was built.

The earliest gatherings of Baptists in the Downton area seem to have taken place in the 1650s on the downs above Wick. It is believed that some of these Baptists were religious exiles returned from Amsterdam, but by 1662 several Downton tradesmen led by Peter Coles, a tanner, were among the local congregation.

The Baptist congregation met formally for the first time in Downton in a cottage in Gravel Close from 1666. It was led by Peter Coles. The group followed General Baptist principles and when these veered towards Unitarianism, a group known as the Particular Baptists broke away in 1734. They met in South Lane in two cottages which have since burnt down, had a regular minister and were in a flourishing state by the end of the 18th century. In 1791 they built a chapel in South Lane and in 1801 appointed a permanent minister. By 1857 the chapel was proving too small and they replaced it with a new one on the same site. At the same time the manse, the minister's house, was extended. The Unitarian Baptists had continued to meet in Gravel Close and in 1715 built a chapel which was replaced in 1835

The Rehoboth Chapel.

by the present building, now the Band Hall. It was used as a chapel until 1935.

The Particular Baptists reunited with the General Baptists in 1894, although the latter continued to use their own chapel in Gravel Close until about 1935. Both congregations then worshipped at the Particular Baptist chapel in South Lane, which is now known as Downton Baptist Church.

What is now a garage and a flat on Lode Hill housed another of Downton's breakaway religious groups. It was formerly a Rehoboth Strict Baptist Chapel. In 1842 a group of Strict Baptists were formed by an orator called Mr. Tiptaft, locally known as 'The Thunderer' and this chapel was founded in 1845 with a permanent pastor, Mr. Jones. He died in 1858 and was not replaced, causing the congregation to gradually dwindle. The chapel was closed by the 1950s and by 1975 had been converted to its current use.

Church attendance

Non-conformists all over the country were persecuted and excluded until, in the words of historian John Chandler, the Toleration Act of 1689 'opened a new chapter ....by removing from the established church the monopoly of legal forms of religious worship and enabling dissenting groups to progress from small bands of persecuted enthusiasts to a respectable, powerful and significant minority in English life.'[11] Religious groups of every kind were encouraged to register their places of meeting and worship with the authorities and the vast majority of these registrations survive for Wiltshire to provide us with a clear indication of the development of non-conformist groups.

We can also ascertain fairly accurately the size of the various congregations in Downton by the mid-nineteenth century from the Religious Census carried out in 1851.[12] Every place of worship was required to fill in a return for the 30th March 1851, listing attendance at all services. Most split the figures into 'General Congregation' and 'Sunday Scholars'. There was also a requirement to provide 'average attendance' in order to take account of possible exceptional days of poor attendance although no evidence had to be provided for these figures so many may have been aspirational. In addition ministers had to give the name of the church, the parish, the date of consecration of the building if after 1800 and the sources of income. Non-conformists were not asked to supply details of income but were asked about the capacity of the building and whether it was used exclusively for worship, as many worshippers in those days met in private dwellings.

Downton had a population of 3898 in 1851. In that year non-conformist congregations accounted for 1693 people which represents just over 43% of the population of the village if taken at face value. In reality multiple attendance was common so it is difficult to estimate the exact number of non-conformists in the village at the time. The authorities reduced the non-conformist figures returned in the census for afternoon attendance by one third and for the evening by two thirds.

The figures are split between the various non-conformist chapels as follows:

Place of Worship			
	AM	PM	Eve
Lode Hill Methodists	180		163
Rehoboth Strict Methodists	88		30
South Lane Baptists	215	175	130
Gravel Close General Baptists	52	70	100
Wesleyan Methodists	80	70	90

By contrast the census return submitted for the Anglican church of St. Laurence looks odd. The vicar, Canon Richard Payne, signed the return as required, but apart from entering approximate figures, failed to give any other details. This contrasts with all other ministers in Downton who filled in their forms meticulously. Also unlike the above, who dated their forms '30th March' Payne entered the date of '21st March'. The figures given by Payne for St. Laurence are:

Place of Worship	AM	PM	Eve
St. Laurence	400	500	

Payne also entered his estimate for the average congregation as 400 in the morning and 500 in the afternoon, in other words exactly the same as his supposed actual figures. The breakdown of the actual figures he entered for the morning service were, 200 for the general congregation and 200 for Sunday scholars and in the afternoon service he entered 300 for the general congregation and 200 for the Sunday scholars, the estimated average figures being identical. It is difficult to accept that these figures were anything other than very broad estimates and the temptation is to go further and suggest that they were overestimates. Even if they are close to the truth, they suggest that only 23% of Downton's population attended Anglican services, in contrast with up to 43% attending non-conformist services. Neither was St.

Laurence filled to capacity. The highest figure of a congregation of 300 in the afternoon would not have filled the church whose capacity has been estimated at approximately 500.

When we compare Anglican attendance in Downton with that of neighbouring parishes the numbers become even more interesting. In Winterslow for example nearly 63% of the village attended Anglican services (population 913, morning attendance 285, afternoon attendance 290). In Whiteparish 40% attended (population 1344, morning attendance 275, afternoon attendance 263). In Redlynch nearly 41% attended (population 1279, morning attendance 257, afternoon attendance 263). In Britford nearly 52% attended (population 938, morning attendance 242, afternoon attendance 244). A comparison with the wider picture tells a similar story. John Elliott in his analysis of worship in Salisbury in 1851 reported that the total Anglican attendance for Wiltshire was 52.2% of the population and the national figure was 47%. Non-conformist worship for the whole of Wiltshire stood at 46.7% and nationally at 48.6%, which makes the Downton non-conformist figures not untypical.[13]

The 1851 Religious Census suggests that attendance at the Anglican St. Laurence church was poor in comparison with regional and national figures. It is difficult to surmise the causes. The vicar of Downton, Richard Payne served the parish for over 40 years (1841-1883). The lychgate at the entrance to the church yard was erected in his memory suggesting a respected minister. But it is possible that he held High Church views because in 1850 he wrote to the *Salisbury Journal* in support of the Oxford Movement regarding the case of the Reverend George Gorham and taking the High Church view that the state could not decide on disputes of religious doctrine.[14] His opinions of the dissenting bodies were apparent when, in the late 1860s and 1870, he wrote several letters to the *Salisbury Journal* strongly critical of dissenters who were campaigning for a ban on religious education in Board schools about to be set up under the 1870 Education Act. He insisted that pupils should be taught according to Anglican principles.[16] In itself this view was not untypical of most Anglicans and was not exclusively held by those of the High Church but the letters could have exacerbated a growing divide between Anglicanism and non-conformism locally.

In one respect Payne was a typical Anglican vicar reflecting the widespread view in the church that the state religion was losing its hold and this was due to social dislocation of industrialisation, urbanisation and political conflict. In the words of John Elliott there was a 'breaking of old ties and customs'.[17] Downton had had its share of social and political change, with the enclosures, the Swing Riots, parliamentary reform and mass emigration but it is difficult to prove whether any of these factors might have contributed to the untypical figures for Anglican worship or whether there was a clash of views with the vicar. The answer may lie in individual personalities. We have seen how Mr. Tiptaft attracted a relatively large congregation to his Rehoboth chapel on Lode Hill. Similarly, the evidence may suggest that Canon Richard Payne had an unsympathetic approach to a changing rural society.

Players

Over the years Downton has developed both a reputation and a capacity for making merry. This could not have happened without a strong sense of community and a small and dedicated number of inhabitants prepared to devote time and effort to providing a broad range of entertainments and activities. In most cases too modest to come forward and be named, the village nevertheless owes them a debt of gratitude for upholding a delightful village tradition.

In former times fairs and markets had a serious commercial purpose as well as providing entertainment. When the bishop of Winchester established the borough of Downton in the 13th century the new main street was deliberately laid out to allow space for a market which was held on Thursdays. In fact the new part of Downton was originally referred to as New Market[11] although the name did not continue and soon the old and new sections were collectively known

A 19th century Cuckoo Fair in the Borough (Margaret Smith)..

as Downton, with the old street known as the High Street and the new market area known as The Borough. The inhabitants of these two areas have been referred to as 'top enders' and 'bottom enders' as long as anyone can remember. The market was probably well patronised in medieval times. It is recorded in 1249 and again in the late 14th century.[12] There is also evidence of a fair in 1289, which existed by custom.[13] The bishop of Winchester permitted this fair to be held on the 'eve, day and morrow of St. Laurence' (9th-11th April) although this too seems to have died out some time later.

By 1703 market activities must have ceased because Charles Duncombe petitioned for their re-instatement. He was successful, but from 1792 none was held.

Sir Joseph Ashe, one of Downton's MPs in the late 17th century, obtained a charter from Charles II conferring on Downton the right to hold two fairs annually, on 23rd April for cattle and pedlars and on 2nd October for sheep and horses.[14] Profits from these fairs were to fund the free school founded by Gyles Eyre. The accounts for these fairs provide a picture of Downton not dissimilar from its modern descendant, the Cuckoo Fair. Stalls were set up and stallholders were charged. Gangs of men were paid to make preparations and they were also provided with what J.H. Bettey refers to as 'food and prodigious quantities of beer'. Animal pens and chicken coops were constructed along each side of The Borough for livestock and fowl.

These biannual fairs continued to be held until the early 20th century. The October fair is reported to have taken place as late as 1917.[15] The April fair may have died out sooner and it is clear that both fairs ceased shortly after the First World War, possibly because improved transport links made it more feasible for people to travel to the Salisbury markets and because annual events held by Downton's Friendly Societies became more important. Of these the Wiltshire Friendly Society and the Ancient Order of Foresters held annual festivals at Whitsuntide. Both involved a church service and a parade, one on Whit Monday and one on Whit Tuesday. The WFS also held a dance and entertainment in the Moot and the Foresters held theirs in Barford Park as the landowner, Lord Radnor, was a key member.

By the turn of the 20th century the list of sports and pastimes available in Downton continued to grow. There was a golf club, a football club and a quoits club and these would soon be followed by a rifle club. Two hunts regularly met in the area, the Wilton Hunt and the Downton Foot Beagles.[16]

As Downton nestled in the beautiful Avon valley many simply took a walk through the water meadows along the river, perhaps with a picnic by New Court, Jiggy Joggy field or Catherine Meadow with its network of streams providing swimming for children and a picturesque setting for courting couples. A much appreciated mix of leisure and self improvement activities was provided by the Unionist Club, when the earl of Radnor opened it in 1902 in part of the old workhouse building. The club provided welcome opportunities to read daily and weekly magazines and newspapers for an increasingly literate populace, many of whom also took a keener interest in current affairs since the extension of the franchise. Membership swelled and a hall and billiard room were later added.[17]

The Downton Band

A key element of many village social events was the Downton Band. Silver bands are a traditional feature of the life of Wiltshire but the early history of bands in Downton is not entirely certain. Bert Giles, a Downton Band member, found that there was an orchestra formed of members of the White Horse Friendly Society in 1870. Giles assumed that this was a forerunner of Downton Band but this is not corroborated by an entry in the Downton Parish Magazine of August 1889 which reported that:

> A Brass Band has been formed by some young men of Downton, who have begun their practices under the tuition of Mr. Davies.

This photograph of Woodfalls Temperance Band is thought to date from the 1880s. The Downton parish magazine of July 16th 1883 describes how this band headed a procession to a service held in Downton. Known names are Charles Mitchell (with whiskers), John Smith (with a sousaphone) and the father of Gilbert Eastman, the Downton basket maker (holding drumsticks). (Margaret Smith).

The Downton band at Breamore in 1908 Back row, left to right: Jack Bailey, Jim Moody, George Bailey, Charlie Chalke, Ernest Bailey, Frank Noble, Fred Blake, Charlie Moody, John Smith.
Middle row: Sam Senior, Walt Bailey, Frank Bundy, Harry Winton.
Front row: Sam Durdle (child) Bert Smith, Walter Bailey, Ralph Bundy, Percy Chalke.
Of these, Ralph Bundy and Harry Winton died in the First World War.
(Don Moody).

> The vicar acts as treasurer. They wish to thank those who have
> kindly contributed to enable them to purchase their instruments.

Mr. Fanner was bandmaster and other founder members included John Smith (1864-1935) and Henry Eastman, who had played in the Woodfalls Band before helping to set up the Downton Band. The Moody family were also very prominent in the band from its early days. Mr. Fanner continued until 1900, after which the position was taken over by Mr. G. Chalke. Later Walter Bailey and then his brother Ernest took the lead until 1923. Ernest served with the band for 60 years. Subsequent bandmasters included Roy Woodford, the church organist, who also noted down some aspects of the history of Downton.

Don Moody remembered that a Downton Home Guard Band was formed during the Second World War. Because of a shortage of players during wartime, the Downton and Woodfalls Band combined and Don Moody played in the band as a 12-year-old in a uniform

The Downton and Woodfalls Home Guard Band in the Second World War. (Don Moody).

which was far too big for him. The other members were in the Home Guard, and included Fishy Hallett, Harold and Stubby Sherwood and Harold Plaskett.[18]

In 1969 the Downton Band took over the old chapel in Gravel Close and in 1977 it became known as the Downton Huntsman Band following brewery sponsorship. It has continued to be a mainstay of Downton's social life and plays at most major village events including the annual Remembrance Sunday Parade and at dawn recitals throughout the village every cold Christmas Day morning.

Youth

The Downton Band benefited its members and its audiences alike, although possibly appealing to more traditional tastes. With the explosion of popular youth culture in the 1950s and 1960s, Downton may have seemed a little too conservative for some, that is until a youth club called the Beebop began to meet in the Unitarian Chapel near Waterside. Local boys were inspired to form groups and perform. Johnny Holgate, a local teacher, headed up Johnny and the Woodworms and another well-known local group was Brian Moon and the Satellites. Newman's Cafe, on the junction between Gravel

The Downton band on stage, probably in the Memorial Hall in the 1950s.
Back row L to R: Geoff Collins, Reg Smith, Jack Moody, Norman Street, Les
Forder, Joe Eastman,
Middle row: Brian Kenley (almost out of picture), Mrs. Street, George Corbin,
Tom Burton, Ray Morgan, Jim Moody, Earn Barter, Bert Giles, Jim Speadbury,
Norman Batten.
Front row: Jack Sherwood, George Spreadbury, Arthur Moody, Roy Woodford,
William Moody, Sid Shutler, George Sherwood.
(Don Moody).

Close and the Borough, was equipped with pinball machines and was
another popular venue especially favoured by bikers from far and
wide. Boxing matches were also organised in the Memorial Hall, often
between youth club teams and young army recruits from Salisbury
Plain.

Carnivals, Pageants and Plays

In a feature about Downton in 2003 the *Salisbury Journal* proclaimed
in its headline, 'Downton has always known how to party'. It reported
that coronations, jubilees and the millennium gave villagers ample
excuses to organise carnivals, pageants and concerts.

Impressive productions and pageants have been held in Downton
since at least the late 19th century. Events staged at the Moot were

On Wednesday, June 22nd, Mr Ben Greets Company will perform
two of Shakespeare's plays:

At 3.40pm, **The Comedy of Errors** and at 8pm, by limelight,
Twelfth Night, in the Ancient Amphitheatre of the Moot.

On Thursday, June 23rd, there will be a Maypole Dance, Concert and
Display of Fireworks. The Entertainment will conclude each evening
with a Torchlight Procession.
The Downton Band will attend both days.

Lawn Tennis etc.   Tea and Refreshments

often extraordinarily ambitious. Programmes and reports in the
Salisbury Journal attest to this fact.[19] The programme of 1898, is an
example.

On this occasion the proceeds helped to pay for repairs to the
church. It was a great success with approximately 3,000 people
attending over the two days. Ben Greet's theatre company was a popular
attraction. Mr. Greet was a well-known actor manager who toured
the country with a company which later included the young Sybil
Thorndike. This young actress was critically acclaimed from an early
age and she appeared in a later Moot production of The Comedy of
Errors, with Ben Greet's company in 1908, playing Adriana. On that
occasion the *Salisbury Journal* noted that she played her part 'with a
sympathetic sense of its strong dramatic qualities'. Downton children
from the Board School and players from Downton Band also took
part regularly in these events and the back stage work and stall holding
were all undertaken by local people. In all events special trains were
laid on from Bournemouth and Salisbury to attract a a large audience.

Ben Greet's was a company of professional actors but amateur
productions have also thrived for well over a hundred and forty years.

The staging of A Comedy of Errors in the Moot in 1908 (Margaret Smith).

The carnival programme 1963 (Downton History Group).

An early example was noted in the 1884 Parish Magazine:

> A Grand Amateur Concert in aid of a fund to pay a nurse to visit the sick. Front row seats cost 2 shillings 6 pence, side seats – 6 pence. Violin players included Miss A.M. Squarey and the leader was Mr. A. Foley.

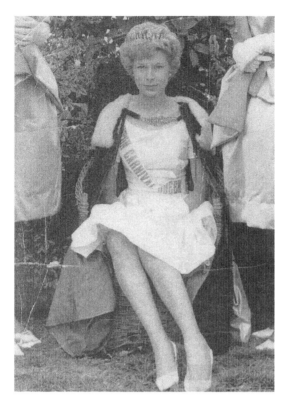

The 1963 Carnival queen, Jackie Bond (Downton History Grouip - Hill Collection).

Coronations and jubilees always provided an excuse for celebration in Downton. This was the case even when the coronation of Edward VII was postponed in June 1902 because the king developed appendicitis. On the scheduled coronation day a tea and some locally planned events went ahead, including a comic football match and a dance. A torchlight parade and a bonfire on Barford Down were postponed until news of the king's recovery on 30th June and these were followed by a procession through the streets, a concert and maypole dancing on 9th August.

Connolly's Fair was set up on the village green once a year between the wars. It was a rare experience for children to experience the thrill of galloping horses on a roundabout, swinging boats and the chance to win a toy from one one of its many stalls.

Since the end of the Second World War, carnivals were held regularly in August. Following several days of competitions and dances the main attraction, anticipated by village schoolchildren, was a long procession of carnival floats, decorated by local businesses and organisations, which wound its way along the length of the village. Accompanying the floats was the Downton Band and a procession of children and adults in fancy dress, with prizes for the best dressed

Children in fancy dress wait to join the carnival procession by Hickman's grain store. The author, as a fortune-teller, 4th from right (not including the donkey!) and next to 'Christine Keeler' (author's collection).

The infamous wheelbarrow race. A young Malcolm Dean peeps out extreme left, next left is Jim Blake. (Downton History Group - Hill Collection).

The DAD's production of *Quiet Weekend*. On the right is a young girl, Frances Hall, who sadly died in 1972 (author's collection).

competitor. A carnival queen was crowned and an adjunct to the carnival procession was a wheelbarrow grand prix in which teams of young men would push each other from the top of the High Street to the bottom of The Borough, stopping at every public house along the way for each to consume a pint of beer. The events often started merrily then turned into quite drunken and rowdy affairs as there were five pubs along the route in the 1960s, the New Inn, the King's Arms, the Three Horseshoes, the White Horse and the Bull, and the friendly rivalry between teams from the top end and the bottom end could become vehement. The annual carnival had died out by the 1970's but was revived to celebrate the millennium. On that occasion an ambitious open air concert was also held in the Memorial Gardens, featuring local people as well as Ceilidh, a local folk group, and Brian Moon and the Satellites. So successful was this event that carnivals and open air concerts were also held to celebrate the Queen's Golden Jubilee in 2002 and her Diamond Jubilee in 2012. All were organised and performed entirely by local people.

In days past, mumming plays had been performed in the open air around the village cross but more recently another outlet for local talent was the Downton Amateur Dramatic Society, known affectionately as the DADs, which was formed in 1969. Its first production was the relatively low key 'Thistle' in a Donkey Field. This was quickly

The 1993 Downton Pageant.

followed by more ambitious productions staged in the Memorial Hall, such as Esther McCracken's farce, *Quiet Weekend*. At the time of writing there still exists an enthusiastic band of amateur actors who regularly perform in the village.

In 1993 a pageant charting Downton's history was written by

The Diamond Jubilee Street Party.

Downton resident Dr. Miranda Whitehead and directed by Peter Waddington. It was performed by local people in the Moot Gardens, with talent and huge enthusiasm and effort making up for any deficiencies in historical accuracy. It was a very popular and widely appreciated historical spectacle.

Downton's revived annual Cuckoo Fair was the brainchild of Peter Waddington, MBE, his wife Shirley and Chris Pitts. Founded in 1980 and based on the idea of the medieval April fair, the Downton Cuckoo Fair was welcomed at a time when the number of shops, businesses and workshops had been in decline.[20] It has had a great social impact on the village. The modern Cuckoo Fair began as a small village event on the greens giving local people an opportunity to rent a table and sell produce and unwanted items. It is so named as it falls on the early May Bank Holiday weekend, just at the time when the first cuckoo is usually heard in Catherine Meadow. Local folklore suggests that the arrival of the cuckoo after the winter was of great significance as it heralded Spring. There is also a local legend which tells of the cuckoo being penned up all year to keep away the colder seasons and that in Downton it was penned in the pound.[21]

Downton Cuckoo Fair has grown into one of the south of England's biggest open air events, welcoming around 15,000 visitors and with

Peter Waddington MBE, founder Downton Cuckoo Fair..

A family picnic, near New Court, between the wars (author's collection).

250 stalls. Greeted enthusiastically by most and less so by a few, the air of anticipation in the days before the event is almost tangible as vast marquees are erected covering most of the village greens. The Borough and High Street are closed to vehicle traffic all day and the village throngs with thousands of visitors. Highlights include maypole dancing, a plastic duck race on a stream, performances by local bands and the crowning of the Cuckoo Princess with a crown of Downton lace. Despite some misgivings that it has become too large and maybe a touch too commercial, it remains a unique event and is generally welcomed as an opportunity for Downton to be on show and to party all day long. More importantly perhaps it remains a powerful symbol of community, hospitality and a love of life which has survived through the ages.

Children bathing at Four Hatches in South Lane shortly after the Second World War. From left to right in the water, Diana Sharp, Nicola Mather, Margaret Smith. Standing on the right pier – Jean Garrett with Pam Garrett seated left. (Margaret Smith).

12

River

Walking northwards along Gravel Close, as one leaves the village and passes New Court farm, a concrete farm track leads to some farm buildings. To the right of that track lies a water course, its straightness a clue to its man-made origin. Kick away the undergrowth at the edge of the track and you will uncover a brick wall, the edge of a canal, which is a vestige of the attempt to make the Hampshire Avon navigable as far as Salisbury in the 17th century. An Act of Parliament, known as the Clarendon Act, was passed in 1664 to allow for the work which was to improve the movement of freight, particularly coal, from the south coast.[1] It was the brainchild of a colourful character, John Taylor, a Thames waterman and pamphleteer. In 1623 he made a journey by sea and river from London to the south coast and then by river to Salisbury. In a subsequent pamphlet he promoted the idea of making the Hampshire Avon navigable although he was not actively involved with the scheme and died in 1653 before work began.[2] Bishop of Salisbury, Seth Ward, was a leading advocate of the project and work began in 1675, with the backing of local businessmen and landowners. It was also financially supported by Salisbury City Corporation, with the idea of reviving the city's fortunes following the collapse of the woollen trade. The project was not a success and the river was only navigable between 1680 and 1695 and again between 1710 and 1720. It was little used and there was a lack of investment in maintenance.[3] All that remains in Downton, apart from a stretch of canalisation between New Court Farm and Charlton, is the vestige of

The vestiges of the straight canal bank next to the footpath between Downton and Charlton.

a wharf on the tannery site. Legal challenges by canoeists to reassert the right to use boats on the Avon in recent times have all failed due to opposition from riparian owners and the fishing lobby. The Clarendon Act which allowed the development of the navigation has never been repealed but the legal right to navigate the river has lapsed.

In the late 17th century Downton, like many other villages situated on flood plains, used a system of water meadows to improve irrigation and stimulate grass growth for animals, principally sheep.

The system necessitates water being diverted via carriers (such as the New Court Carrier north of the village) by a system of hatches and sluice gates usually made of elm or oak and directed along channels, known as floaters or gutters, on the tops of man-made ridges in the fields. Water runs off these ridges and down the panes, as the slopes of the ridges are known. By a network of drains or furrows in the dips the water then returns to the river. Grass growth is stimulated in the early Spring by this irrigation, principally because the water temperature is often higher in the winter months than the air temperature, though this fact may not have been appreciated at the time, only that it appeared to work. Irrigation served to promote an "early bite" when farmers could return animals to the fields earlier after winter. Similarly the system served to lengthen the grass growing season in the autumn. The water warmed the grass and added nutrients such as nitrogen to the soil whilst sheep helped break up the soil and their dung added fertiliser. The field systems were operated and maintained by 'drowners' who worked the water hatches for the benefit of their flocks.

The late 1600s and early 1700s were a time of great agricultural improvement throughout England. Medieval farming practices had controlled livestock husbandry quite strictly through manorial customs enforced by manor courts though there had been little attempt to improve stock through selective breeding. Thus by today's standards, livestock were small and the system of open field farming restricted the yield of arable land because no allowance could be made for innovative farmers to improve. Overall there was little opportunity for the small farmer to do anything other than continue the inefficient methods of his father and grandfather before him, although there was an increase in arable farming on the chalk down lands to meet increased demand from a rising population.[4] Daniel Defoe commented in his tour through England in the 1720s that in Wiltshire, 'many thousands of acres of the carpet ground being of late years turned into arable'.[5] Sheep still grazed on the upper down lands and in the valley there was dairy farming and horse breeding.

One of the major problems with early farming was that a farmer could never produce enough winter fodder to keep the majority of his livestock alive through the winter, so an autumn slaughter was a

Catherine Meadow.

necessity. Therefore the innovation of water meadows to prolong the grass growing season was an important step towards improving the well-being of livestock and their keepers.

The water meadow which forms Catherine Meadow in Downton was the project of Joseph Ashe, resident of New Court and the Member of Parliament for Downton between 1678 and 1685. Originally from Somerset, he settled in Twickenham and bought Cambridge Park, Middlesex. On 19th September 1660, after the restoration, he was created a baronet by King Charles II as a reward for his loyalty to Charles I in the Civil War. Ashe first entered the House of Commons in 1670 and when in Downton he resided at New Court.

The Catherine water meadows demanded an elaborate pattern of channels, ditches, sluices and hatches to be constructed, allowing the flow of the nutrient rich chalk streams over the grazing lands. Considerable financial outlay was required for the work which is why it needed a man of financial means, such as Sir Joseph Ashe, to invest in this new method. Ashe charged his steward, John Snow, with the task of overseeing the work. He frequently complained to his steward that the cost was double the original estimate, to which the steward answered that the work was complex but the reward was considerable. John Snow was clearly a remarkable man and was a great enthusiast as far as water meadows were concerned. He supervised the whole project which was begun in 1665. It involved not only designing the layout but negotiating with other landowners and costing the whole operation. More than forty complex agreements were reached with neighbouring landowners, including arrangements for access for

The bridge and hatches over the New Court Carrier, as they were in the 1950s (WI Scrapbook)..

horses carrying timber, stone, chalk, bricks and straw to build and repair hatches and sluices. He made hastily scribbled reports to Ashe, often justifying expenses, and frequently had to travel to London to meet him, a journey which took two days. For example on February 19th 1690 Snow wrote:

Spent the whole (day) riding up February and 18 days – 7s 8d.[6]

Sir Joseph took a close interest in the work but at times lost patience with Snow. On 22nd March 1690 he wrote to him saying:

I have your tedious letter of the 15th and I thinke this Cursed Wateringe hath given me ten tymes the trouble that all the other concerns of my life hath done.[7]

John Snow pointed out the benefits of developing the water meadows as follows:

Argument to shew what greate profitt may redound to the owners of the Land upon a free improvement, by drowninge wateringe or draynage as followeth:
By so doeinge there will be a greater increase in hay.
There will be a greate increase in cattle.
Thereby will be a greater increase in Corne.
There will be a greater increase of Hay …
Haye beinge plenty men may keepe more Cattle whereby their ground may be much better and improved.
Their ground being thus bettered and improved there will be a greater increase of Corne and there after Grasse of their grounds thus improved will be of great benefitt for the feeding of Cattle both fatt and also for butter and cheese.[8]

Snow's argument focuses on the production of milk, cheese and beef for which their was growing demand due to an increased population and easy access to markets in Salisbury and Southampton. Another compelling reason for the construction of water meadows was that they at least doubled the value of the land. One section of 194 acres was said to be worth £174 a year before watering and £428 after watering.[9] No doubt this was why the Avon was soon completely 'meadowed' following Ashe's example, from Salisbury to Downton.

An oral tradition has long suggested that Dutch engineers or prisoners of war were responsible for the construction work but Nancy Steele suggested that the belief came about because some of

Fishermen on the River Avon south of Downton in the 1950s (Margaret Smith).

the ironwork on the hatches bears the inscription 'B.DUTCH WAR'. Benjamin Dutch was in fact a smith and engineer from Warminster.[10]

The accounts and letters of Sir Joseph Ashe and John Snow provide a rich insight into the establishment and management of one of Downton's principal features. The water meadows continued to operate until the second half of the 20th century and for over 350 years the work of the drowners was crucial in ensuring the flow of water through the meadows was correctly controlled to provide maximum benefit for pasture. When the system finally fell into disuse in the 1950's, the ditches and carriers slowly filled with debris and the culverts became blocked, although the dips and rises of the gutters and panes are still visible and the meadows continued to provide many hours of pleasure for local children who delighted in paddling in them.

The meadows have never been re-instated as they have in Harnham on the outskirts of Salisbury and their state of disrepair was considered by many residents as a factor which contributed to the flooding of the village in recent times even though experts disagreed on the impact.

Throughout history Downton has been famed for its fishing. The river holds rich stocks of coarse fish as well as trout and salmon. Freshwater crayfish were also common until recent times. The right to fish in the Avon belonged to the lord of the manor or whoever held the lease of the manor at the time, since medieval times. For example John Stockman, as the owner of Barford park, held the fishing rights from Standlynch to Weirgaps from 1575. After the Second World War the Bull Hotel bought the fishing rights to a long stretch of the river south of Downton and became famous as a fishing hotel. In the 1960s, owned and managed by the Scott-Newmans, it was the hotel of choice for amateur fishermen in the world of show business, including the singer Billy Fury and the comedian Eric Morecambe. A more recent development on a commercial level has been the establishment of Trafalgar Fish Farm.

The fresh chalky nutrient-rich River Avon may have been regarded as a blessing by those who deliberately flooded the water meadows for improved yields but this contrasts sharply with the suffering endured by generations of Downton residents subjected to regular flooding events of their homes. Floods were a common occurrence particularly in The Borough by virtue of its proximity to the river and the low flat alluvial flood plain. The earliest habitation, including the Roman villa, was sited just above the flood plain as was the old village centre near the church. It was the medieval development of what is now The Borough, west of the old village, in the 13th century, which has always been most prone to flooding and this was probably one of the main factors affecting Downton's failure to develop into a successful town. Quite why this was not appreciated when the borough was founded is a mystery but it may have something to do with the ambient weather in the 13th century. It is possible that the area had not flooded for some time before the establishment of the borough.

Downton flooded regularly, the earliest recorded flood being in 1606. Floods varied in severity with sometimes only a handful of cottages affected, sometimes most of the lower village. Many of the smaller events went unrecorded, even in recent times, except by

The flood of 1915 (Margaret Smith).

those who remembered them through personal experience. In recent times the most serious floods recorded were those in 1915, 1960 and 2000. Of these the 1915 flood was particularly devastating, not only because it happened during the First World War but because it affected 125 properties and was considered the worst flood since Napoleonic times.[11] It was also the first flood to have been widely recorded by the camera.

Climate change may explain why floods became increasingly frequent towards the end of the 20th century. In 2002 BBC local news reported that the flood which occurred in December 2000 flooded forty properties and forced seventeen families to seek alternative accommodation. It followed four floods in the previous ten years.[12]

The human cost was substantial. Downtonians met each crisis of rising water levels with courage and good humour but a cheerful facade often concealed enormous stress. To see water rising through the floor or creeping under a door was traumatic enough but the clean up was as bad and sometimes it was months before normal life could be resumed.

The situation became so serious that, following the floods in 2000 and with much pressure by local councillors and the local MP Robert Key, Downton was granted Special Case Status by the Government and was made a priority by the Environment Agency. Following public consultation and emergency work which included clearing the New Court Carrier and the Bunny, a scheme of flood defence work costing £2.5million commenced in December 2003. For almost a year, Downton swarmed with contractors, whose headquarters were established behind the Co-operative store. Some villagers endured

The flood of 1915 (Margaret Smith).

Aerial photographs of the 2000 flood (Environment Agency).

bulldozers tearing up their gardens to lay pipes and foundations for a flood defence wall. By the summer of 2004 work was complete, with a wall on the west bank of the river north and south of the Catherine Bridge, earth banking to protect houses to the west of the meadow and the installation of a pumping station in Green Lane to divert ground and surface water into the river. Widening the Catherine Bridge, where water had often backed up when levels were high, was considered but rejected due to objections from the conservation department of the Salisbury District Council.

The Downton Flood Defence Scheme was formally opened in 2004 heralding a new era for Downton.

Conclusion

A single volume, written for the general reader can never include every detail of the history of a community but my hope is that I have captured a meaningful narrative and the most important themes. Very few, if any, historians achieve a definitive history, not least because there will always be evidence lying undiscovered or unstudied. This book seeks not to be definitive but is merely a step in a process of discovery. There have been various previous publications on the history of Downton, several of which have repeated factual errors from one to the other. I have striven for both accuracy and inspiration; accuracy in that facts have been verified as far as possible, inspiration in that this book may hopefully help others in the future to conduct deeper research into aspects of village history or their own family history. There is little doubt that there are many documents relating to this South Wiltshire village still waiting to be studied in greater depth and the task of the local and family historian is gradually becoming easier as more material is catalogued, published and put on the internet.

Two examples of archives which deserve further study are the Radnor papers, yet to be fully catalogued at the time of publication, and the Winchester Pipe Rolls, the records of the Bishops of Winchester, still to be fully translated from medieval Latin. The Radnor papers, held in the Wiltshire and Swindon History Centre, are being catalogued at the time of writing. Only two Winchester Pipe Rolls, held in the Hampshire Record Office, have been fully translated, those dated 1301-2 and 1409-10. The rolls are annual enrolled accounts running in broken series from 1208-9 to 1457-8 and thereafter in volumes until 1710-11. They are among the most complete medieval documents in existence. I have sampled them and looked at previous academic papers which made use of them but their full study is beyond the scope of this work. Regarding oral history there are undoubtedly Downton people, waiting in the wings, who know more than I, on certain areas. I spoke to many but not all because the local historian, whilst having duty to record memories before they are lost, is reliant

Conclusion

on volunteered information. If this book inspires further interest in Downton's rich past and helps to define the community, as all history should, then it will have succeeded.

Appendix 1
Winchester Scholars from Downton

Edward Jay or Not, scholar admitted 1394

Nicholas Helyer or Upton, scholar admitted 1408

Thomas Ryngwode, scholar admitted 1414, left 1416

William Strode, scholar admitted 1419, left 1422

William Body, scholar admitted 1433

John Martin, scholar admitted 1436

John Dogoode, scholar admitted 1458; later a fellow of Win
  Coll 1475

John Brownsopp, scholar admitted 1459

John Mapull, scholar admitted 1468, but left later the same
  year

William Borgh, scholar admitted 1460

John Chypenham, scholar admitted 1465

Richard Wyllys, scholar admitted 1467

Robert Byryet, scholar admitted 1472, age 15

John Crowche, scholar admitted 1474, age 13

George Rede, scholar admitted 1475, age 12

Henry Mompesson, scholar admitted 1476, aged 11

Robert Mapull, scholar admitted 1500, age 12

John Iryssh, scholar admitted 1514, age 14

Charles Matthews, scholar admitted 1546, age 10

Erasmus William, scholar admitted 1566, age 13

John Hobbs, scholar admitted 1633, age 12

Information provided from Winchester College Archives

Appendices

Appendix 2
Downton MPs

1295	John Spede	Richard de la Sale
1298	Reginald Dt. Aula	John Whitthorn
1300	Roger de Portsmouth	Wh. Leicester
1304	Roger de Large	John Ervye
1306	John de Downton	
1311	Robert de Wryere	William Osgood
1312	John le Cove	John Arny
1313	Walter Nymethalf	Roger de Portsmouth
1314	Nicholas de Mareshal	William de Whytham
1318	William Rotarius	Henry le Drapier
1319	..........Norreys	Walter le Whlere
1323	John Curtoys	Nicholas Laverynge
1325	John Curtoys	Nicholas le Cove
1326	Edward de Tarente	Nicholas de Becklesnade
1328	Henricus le Meyre	Stephanus de Regate
1360	Ricardus Whithorn	Johannes Meyer
1362	Johannes Dryewods	Willielmus Benert
1364	Willielmus Wartier	Johannes Willeymn
1413	Johannes Brut	Thomas Knyf
1441	Johannes Whitesemede	Raduiphus Lygh
1446	Johannes Brekenok	Johannes Bailey
1448	Johannes Lawley	Andreas Sparowe

1449	Johannes Rokes	Robertus Tilleney
1450	Walterus Bergn	Johannes Wynge
1452	Radulfus Alye	Thomas Wells
1455	Edwardus Ashwell	Willielmus Brigg
1459	Johanness Wolfe	Thomas Danvers
1467	Thomas Wells	Radulphus Alegh
1472	Thomas Damers	Richard Jaye
1477	Thomas Damers	Richard Jaye
1529	Nicholas Hare	William Horwood
1553	John Norris	John Bamshaw
1554	James Bassit	John Norris
1554	John Bekynsale	William Borne
1555	Henry White	Thomas White
1557	Thomas White	Thomas Girdler
1558	John Stone	Thomas Girdler
1562	Tristram Matthew	Henry Kingsmill
1570	George Penruddocke	Knt. Henry Cooke
1572	William Darrell	Edward Senitlowe
1584	Thomas Wilke	Thomas Cosin
1586	Thomas Gorges	Thomas Wilks
1588	Richard Cosin	Lawrence Thompson
1592	John Goldwell	Thomas Willowby
1597	Robert Turner	George Powell
1601	Thomas Penruddocke	Knt. Edward Baker
1603	Sir Carew Raleigh	William Stockman
1614	Sir Carew Raleigh	William Hendon
1620	Sir Carew Raleigh	Sir Thomas Hinton
1623	Sir William Dddington Jnr.	Sir Clipsy Crew
1625	Edward Herbert	Sir William Doddingon
1625	Edward Herbert	Sir Clipsy Crew

1628	Edward Herbert	Sir Benjamin Rudyard
1640	Sir Edward Griffin	William Eyre
1641	Sir Edward Griffin	Alexander Thistlethwayte
1658	Thomas Fitzjames	William Coles
1660	Giles Eyre	John Elliott
1661	Gilbert Raleigh	Walter Bockland
1678	Maurice Bockland	Sir Joseph Ashe
1681	Maurice Bockland	Sir Joseph Ashe
1685	Maurice Bockland	Sir Charles Raleigh
1688	Maurice Bockland	Sir Charles Raleigh
1690	Maurice Bockland	Sir Charles Raleigh
1695	Charles Duncombe	Sir Charles Raleigh
1698	John Eyre	Carew Raleigh
1700	John Eyre	Carew Raleigh
1701	Sir James Ashe	Carew Raleigh
1702	Sir James Ashe	Sir Charles Duncombe
1705	John Eyre	Sir Charles Duncombe
1707	John Eyre	Sir Charles Duncombe
1708	John Eyre	Sir Charles Duncombe
1710	John Eyre	Sir Charles Duncombe
1711	Thomas Duncombe	Sir Charles Duncombe
1713	John Eyre	John Sawyer
1771	James Hayes	Richard Crofts
1774	Thomas Duncombe	Thomas Dummer
1775	Sir Philip Hales	John Cooper
1779	Hon. Barth. Bouverie	Robert Shafto
1780	Hon. Henry S. Conway	Robert Shafto
1784	Hon. Edward Bouverie	William Scott
1785	Hon. Henry S. Conway	Robert Shafto
1786	Hon. Edward Bouverie	Hon. W.S. Conway
1790	Hon. Barth. Bouverie	Sir William Scott

1796	Hon. Edward Bouverie	Sir William Scott
1801	Viscount Folkstone	Hon. J. Ward
1802	Hon. Edward Bouverie	Lord de Blaquiere
1803	Viscount Marsham	
1806	Hon. Duncombe Bouverie	Hon. Barth. Bouverie
1807	Hon. Barth. Bouverie	Sir Thomas Plumer
1812	Sir T.B. Pechell	Edward Golding
1818	Viscount Folkstone	Sir William Golding
1820	Hon. Barth. Bouverie	Sir T.B. Pechell
1826	T.E.G.B. Estcourt	Robert Southey
1827	Hon. Barth. Bouverie	Alexander Powell
1830	James Brougham	Chas. Shaw Lefevre
1831	James Brougham	Thomas Creevy
1832	Hon. Philip Playdell-Bouverie	

Appendix 3
Notes on Customs and Usage in Downton

1 Custom of the Manor is that the youngest son and youngest daughter shall inherit the lands called Bondlands and Boardlands though "Usage" seems to contradict this by the document then saying that the Eldest daughter shall inherit;

2 Custom is that the eldest son and eldest daughter shall inherit lands known as Knightamhold;

3 Custom is that if a husband be admitted (?) in his lifetime then the wife so long as she shall so long keep herself sole and chaste shall enjoy her widow's estate (without paying a fine ie a capital payment) – penalty is forfeiture of her holding

4 The document recites the forfeiture provisions ie felling of timber on a copyhold estate without licence

5 Any cattle not marked or branded straying onto the Lord of the Manor's land shall be forfeited to the Lord

6 A tenant shall lose his land if he does not answer the third proclamation (at three successive courts), even if he comes at the first and second.

7 The Lord (of the manor) shall have the custody of an infant heir or heiress with their lands during their minority

8 Customary tenants claims;- turf, heath and furze to be cut and likewise to earth dug to make brick and digging of chalk to make lime (bush and furze for burning, subject to the Lords licence plus digging of forest stone sand and earth for reparation

9 Customary tenants rights about the drawing of the flood hatches at the mill from 4pm on Saturday until 8am Monday (presumably to drain the water meadows above the mill, to allow cattle back on the land?)

Appendices

10 Tenants' claim from time immemorial the right to timber to repair Katherine bridge, and St Laurence Church (paying four pence for the marking of each tree)

11 Tenants 'claim that the mills in Downton are customary mills and that tenants ought to grind their corn paying the usual toll

12 Tenants' claim- to have four pound drifts a year (not understood!)

13 Recital of rents payable in the villages, including Downton eg rent due for fishing from Downton Mill to Stanlynch (sic)

From a typed copy of an 'old parchment' (undated) WSA

Appendix 4
Names Listed on Downton War Memorial

First World War

Percy J. Aylett
Frederick W. Bailey
Ernest Batchelor
Frederick Batchelor
Reuben Batchelor
Frederick Bennett
Edward Blake
Charles Bishop
Edward St. L. Bonvalot
Ralph Bundy
Bob Bundy
Whittaker Coombes
Aubrey G.N. Dickenson
Prince L. Eastman
George Elliott
George Forder
Evelyn P. Graves
William Gunstone
Arthur Haydon
William Haydon
George Hobbs
Geoffrey Hunt
Arthur T. Joliffe
Arthur Keeley
Charles Keely
William Kingsbury
William Mitchell

Percy Moody
Fred Moody
Alfred E. Morgan
Walter Mouland
Albert G.K. Musslewhite
Fred Newman
Reginald J. Nicklen
Harry W. Noble
Albert E. Patience
Arthur A. Steward
Harry Senior
Albert Shepherd
Ernest Smith
Edward Swanborough DCM
Arthur Viney
Harry Winton
George Wyndham

Second World War

Richard Crisp
Cecil J. Grace: Died as a prisoner
of war in Austria.
Cecil J. F.Morgan
Cecil H. W.Phillips
Henry E. Phillips
Arthur S. Priddice

Appendices

William F.G.Reynolds
Percy. D. Ridout
Violet Shelly
William G. Stickley

Korea
John Reedham Erskine
<u>Suez</u>
Peter William

Appendix 5
Migrants from Downton to Canada

1835
Jas King, wife, 2 children and 2 adults with 4 children
J. Pracey or Pressey, wife, 2 children and 1 adult and 3 children
Jas. Chalke, wife and 5 children
Henry Higgs
E. Bundy
Jas. Perry
Chas. Bundy

1836 Males

First Name	Surname	Age
George	Alexander	17
Thomas	Allen	20
William	Bampton	38
James	Bampton	6
George	Barrow	28
Henry	Barrow	9
Thomas	Barrow	2
Isaac	Barter	42
Frederick	Barter	11
Henry	Barter	6
John	Barter	4
James	Biddlecombe	44

Appendices

First Name	Surname	Age
George	Biddlecombe	17
Henry	Biddlecombe	12
Charles	Biddlecombe	6
William	Bishop	29
William	Bishop	18
George	Bundy	21
Samuel	Bundy	60
Cornelius	Bundy	13
Mark	Bundy	7
Daniel	Bundy	56
Mark	Bundy	18
Jacob	Bundy	12
Thomas	Chalke	32
Charles	Chalke	8
James	Champ	36
William	Champ	17
Edmund	Champ	9
George	Champ	6
Arthur	Champ	
George	Compton	6
Henry	Deere	18
James	Dredge	30
Joseph	Dredge	31
Henry	Dredge	9
William	Dredge	4
Johanthan	Dredge	19
Thomas	Dredge	22
Samuel	Eastman	18
William	Edmonds	35
John	Edmonds	12

First Name	Surname	Age
Charles	Edmonds	10
George	Edmonds	7
Henry	Edmonds	3
Philip	Foe	45
Edmond	Foe	6
Edmond	Foe	22
Edmund	Forder	21
George	Forder	22
William	Forder	15
Charles	Frampton	20
Charles	Friar	19
Henry	Friar	20
Michael	Futcher	17
George	Futcher	18
Joseph	Gauntlett	35
Joseph	Gauntlett	12
James	Gauntlett	8
Henry	Gilbert	18
James	Goulding	33
Henry	Goulding	4
George	Goulding	1
John	Harrington	33
Stephen	Harris	17
John	Harris	23
Joseph	Higgs	55
George	Higgs	15
WIlliam	Higgs	13
Francis	Higgs	11
Charles	Higgs	8
Henry	Hudson	19

Appendices

First Name	Surname	Age
Joseph	Jellyman	50
James	Jellyman	13
Richard	Jellyman	10
Joseph W.	Jellyman	9
George	Jellyman	8
Alfred	Jellyman	8 mon
James	Jennings	42
Silas	Jennings	18
Robert	Jennings	9
Absalom	Jennings	20
Charles	King	26
Charles	King	26
Charles	King	3
Silas	King	17
Richard	Latty	17
Henry	Latty	19
George	Light	49
James	Light	27
Charles	Light	15
Henry	Light	10
George	Light	8
Lazarus	Light	5
Oran	Light	3 mon
John	Light	21
Frank	Light	1
Charles	Light	18
James	Moody	40
Charles	Moody	17
William	Moody	16
William	Mussell	16

First Name	Surname	Age
William	Noyse	17
John	Poore	15
Charles	Poore	13
Joseph	Poore	10
Henry	Poore	32
George	Pressey	38
Henry	Pressey	14
Phineas	Pressey	11
Frederick	Pressey	7
George	Pressey	6 mon
Thomas	Pretty	34
Henry	Pretty	11
James	Prince	47
Abraham	Prince	16
Obiah	Prince	9
John	Prince	6
Thomas	Small	34
Charles	Small	13
James	Small	10
William	Small	4
Stephen	Swayne	20
Henry	Thom	34
William	Webb	50
John	Webb	11
Silas	Webb	23
Sidney	Webb	21
James	Weeks	22
William	Weeks	2
George	Weeks	3 mon
James	Westcombe	17

Appendices

First Name	Surname	Age
William	Westcombe	19

1836 Females

Ellen	?	4
?	?	6
	Allen	19
Sarah	Bampton	40
Mary	Bampton	4
Sarah	Bampton	2
Elizabeth	Barrow	30
Ann	Barrow	4
Anne	Barter	32
Jane	Barter	8
Harriet	Barter	
Elsey	Biddlecombe	41
Hannah	Biddlecombe	18
Harriet	Bishop	27
Ann	Bishop	7
Elizabeth	Bishop	5
Clarissa	Bishop	2
Mary	Bundy	25
Fanny	Bundy	5
Mary Ellen	Bundy	3
Ethelinda	Bundy	1
Ann	Bundy	45
Harriet	Bundy	19
Jemima	Bundy	10
Mary	Bundy	53
Fanny	Bundy	22
Harriet	Bundy	21

First Name	Surname	Age
Martha	Bundy	16
Mary	Chalk	32
Eliza	Champ	35
Clarissa	Champ	13
Hannah	Dale	40
Matilda	Dale	11
Eliza	Dredge	24
Kesia	Dredge	31
Charlotte	Dredge	1
Sarah	Edmonds	13
Sarah	Foe	40
Eliza	Foe	14
Harriet	Foe	18
Ann	Gauntlet	35
Ann	Gauntlet	14
Elizabeth	Gauntlet	3
Ann	Goulding	40
Mary	Goulding	9
Harriet	Goulding	6
Mary	Higgs	43
Jane	Higgs	7
Sarah	Higgs	3
Frances	Jellyman	43
Frances	Jellyman	12
Mary Ellen	Jellyman	5
Rosanna	Jennings	40
Maria	Jennings	7
Mary Ann	Jennings	1mon
Anne	King	30
Letitia	King	1
Ann	King	37

Appendices

First Name	Surname	Age
Charlotte	King	18
Mary	Light	42
Sarah	Light	13
Thursa	Light	3
Hannah	Light	37
Elizabeth	Light	21
Elizabeth	Moody	40
Sarah	Moody	2
Jane	Moody	69
Louisa	Moody	17
Mary Ann	Poore	22
Mary	Pressey	37
Ann	Pressey	4
Sarah	Pretty	37
Charlotte	Pretty	13
Elizabeth	Pretty	7
Ann	Pretty	2
Anne	Prince	45
Kesia	Prince	11
Rosalinda	Prince	
Mary	Shergold	17
Mary	Small	34
Hannah	Thom	30
Martha	Webb	38
Rhoda	Webb	11
Mary	Webb	4
Martha	Webb	4
Naomi	Webb	24
Emily	Webb	8 mon
Elizabeth	Webb	22
Elizabeth	Weeks	23

Notes

The following abbreviations are used in the notes:

VCH	Victoria County History.
WAM	Wiltshire Archaeological and Natural History Magazine (Wiltshire Studies).
WRS	Wiltshire Record Society.
WSA	Wiltshire and Swindon Archives (at WSHC).
WSHC	Wiltshire and Swindon History Centre, Chippenham.

Chapter 1

1. *VCH Wiltshire* vol. XI.
2. Interview with Margaret Smith.
3. The earliest human remains in Britain date from 700,000 years ago and were found in East Anglia.
4. Marr *A: History of the World* (2012).
5. *VCH Wiltshire*, vol. XI, and Thomas N: *Excavation and Field Work in Wiltshire*, 1956. WAM 56 (1956).
6. Rahtz P.A: *Neolithic and Beaker Sites at Downton*, Salisbury. WAM 58 (1960).
7. *VCH Wiltshire* vol. XI.
8. Salisbury Museum.
9. Cunliffe B: *Danebury: Anatomy of an Iron Age Hill Fort* (1983).
10. Caesar J: *De Bello Gallico*.
11. Tacitus: *Agricola* Book 1.

Chapter 2

1. I use the term 'Saxons' loosely to refer to a number of tribes which invaded Britain from Northern Europe at this time. Sometimes referred to as 'Anglo Saxons', they gave their name to 'England', by which name I refer to this country hereafter.
2. I use the term 'Britain' to refer to the country after the 410AD Roman withdrawal and before we can safely refer to it as England, i.e when Anglo Saxon rule in firmly established. The term 'British' and 'Britons' refers to the native people in the Dark Ages, in contrast to the Saxon invaders. In the Downton area it is interesting to note the mix of place-names, some of Saxon and some of British origin; for example Avon is British, Downton is Saxon.
3. Local amateur historian, Michael Slade, in his self-published booklet,

Downton and Cerdic, asserted that British chieftain Arthur fought near Downton. Neither historians nor archaeologists have proof of Arthur's existence, let alone his presence locally. Slade's work must be discounted as fantasy. Neither do any early writers who mention him, such as Nennius or Geoffrey of Monmouth link him with the Avon Valley at any point.

[4] *Anglo-Saxon Chronicle*.

[5] The Downton W.I. Scrapbook (1956) mentions the destruction of a tumulus to construct the ornamental gardens.

[6] I am grateful to Emeritus Professor David Hinton of Southampton University for guidance on Charford.

[7] www.southwilts.com/site/St-Birinus-Church/index.

[8] Moot House and Gardens, *Country Life*, January 9th 1909.

[9] Squarey E.P: *The Moot and its Traditions* (1906).

[10] Rahtz P.A: 'Saxon and Medieval Features in Downton'. *WAM* 59 (1961).

[11] Finberg H.P.R: *Early Charters of Wessex* (1964).

[12] *VCH Wiltshire* vol. XI.

[13] Wright G.N: *Roads and Trackways of Wessex* (1988).

[14] Waymouth D: *Downton, 7000 Years of an English Village* (1999).

[15] Rev. Du Boulay Hill A: 'The Saxon Boundaries of Downton, Wiltshire', *WAM* 36 (1909-10).

[16] Schama S: *History of Britain*, vol. 1 (2000).

Chapter 3

[1] www.history.wiltshire.gov.uk.

[2] www.domesdaymap.co.uk/Downton and *VCH Wiltshire* vol. XI. These figures differ from the Downton Heritage Trail booklet (2009).

[3] *VCH Wiltshire* vol. IV.

[4] www.englishheritage.org.uk.

[5] Giles J.A. (ed.) *William of Malmesbury: History of the Norman Kings* (1847).

[6] Bettey J. H: *Wessex from AD 1000* (1986).

[7] www.parliament.uk.

[8] The Bishop of Winchester was one of only a few citizens besides the King who had the right to raise his own taxes and create his own law court in London. He even had his own prison known as "The Clink".

[9] Hinton D: 'Tannery House Archaeological Evaluation': *Wessex Archaeology Report* No: 463, unpub.

[10] *VCH Wiltshire* vol. XI.

[11] Riall N: 'Hampshire in the Anarchy, 1142-1153. The Role of Bishop Henry of Blois.' *Hatcher Review* vol. 4 no. 37 1994.

[12] Hinton D.

[13] Howlett R: *Chronicles of the Reigns of Stephen, Henry II and Richard I* (1884).

Chapter 4

[1] *VCH Wiltshire* vol. XI and British Library Egerton MS 241.

[2] Beresford M.W: 'The Six New Towns of the Bishop of Winchester, 1200-

1255'. *Medieval Archaeology* 3 (1959). The other five towns apart from Downton are Alresford, Hindon, Overton, Newtown (Hants.) and Newtown (I.O.W.).

3   The street is referred to as 'The Borough', whereas the term 'borough' is used in this book when referring to the administrative unit or town of Downton between 1208 and 1832.

4   WSA uncatalogued, accession number 4190/2013. George Futcher was appointed as both Bailiff and Hayward. He is buried St. Laurence churchyard.

5   Titow J Z: *English Rural Society* (1969).

6   Titow J.Z: *English Rural Society* (1969).

7   *VCH Wiltshire* vol. XI.

8   www.downtonbuildings.org

9   *Oxford Dictionary of National Biography* (2004).

10 Floyer J.K: 'Passages from the History of Downton' *WAM* 29 (1896-7).

11 www.downtonbuildings.org and *VCR Wiltshire* vol. XI.

12 Local folklore.

13 *VCH Wiltshire* vol. IV.

14 Leggett E: 'The Black Death on the Estates of the Bishop of Winchester', in Vinogradoff, P. *Oxford Studies in Social and Legal History* (1916) and Titow J.Z: 'Land and Population on the Bishop of Winchester's Estates', PhD thesis, Cam. (1962).

15 Winchester Pipe Rolls (Hampshire Archives, 11M59/B1/101 and 11M59/B1/102). Sections on Downton translated by Peter Eaves.

16 Page M. (ed.) *The Pipe Roll of the Bishopric of Winchester 1409-10* (1999).

17 *VCH Wiltshire* vol. IV.

18 Page M. (ed.) *The Pipe Roll of the Bishopric of Winchester, 1409-10* (1999).

19 Tithes were a tax, usually in kind, paid to the church.

20 A rector is entitled to tithes whereas a vicar is not.

21 Courtesy of Winchester College Archives. For a list of Downton scholars at Winchester see Appendix 1.

Chapter 5

1   www.britishlistedbuildings.co.uk

2   Foxe's Book of Martyrs was a contemporary work describing the martyrdom of Protestants under Mary's reign. For this reason its anti-Catholic slant should be taken into account when reading such stories.

3   Sir Christopher Hatton briefly owned the Breamore estate before selling it to the Dodington family who built Breamore House.

4   This information courtesy of Winchester College Archives.

5   National Portrait Gallery.

6   Cunnington B. H. (ed.) *Records of the County of Wilts, being extracts from the Quarter Sessions Great Rolls of the 17th Century* (1932).

7   Chandler J: *Endless Street* (1983).

8   Waymouth states in *Downton, 7000 years of an English Village*, that Charles I stayed in Moot House, but it was not built until c.1700, Charles I was executed in 1642.

9   Standlynch Park was built in 1733 by Sir Peter Vandeput on the site of Standlynch Manor. In 1813 it was purchased by the nation, renamed Trafalgar House and settled with the heirs of Admiral Lord Nelson.

10   Slocombe I. (ed.) 'Wiltshire Quarter Sessions Order Book 1642-1654'. (*WRS*, vol 67, 2014) ref. no. 469.

11   Ibid. ref. no. 560.

12   *Historical Manuscripts Commission: Report on Manuscripts in Various Collections*, vol. I

13   See chapter 4. The town-crier's bell was donated to Downton Society.

14   Quoted from the memorial to William Stockman in St. Laurence's Church.

15   For more information on the water meadows see chapter 12.

16   See chapter 12.

17   For the full story of the Avon navigation see chapter 12.

18   Courtesy of the Ashe family blog: ashefamily.info.

19   For more about the Squarey family and Moot House see chapters 7 and 8 and 11.

20   www.battlefieldstrust.com.

21   I am grateful to Professor John Morrill of Cambridge University for this information.

Chapter 6

1   Great Bedwyn, Cricklade, Heytesbury, Hindon, Ludgershall and Wootton Bassett in Wiltshire each sent two MPs to parliament and were approximately the same size as Downton. Courtesy of Terry Bracher: The Rotten Boroughs of Wiltshire, WSHC lecture 2014.

2   Quoted in www.historyofparliamentonline.org.

3   www.historyofparliamentonline.org.

4   The Ballot Act was passed in 1872. Before this voting was by a public show of hands.

5   The Bouveries were descended from Huguenot merchants who had fled to England in the 16th century. William de Bouverie purchased Longford Castle in 1717.

6   The website www.historyofparliamentonline.org contains a full explanation of the case. It was also recorded by Conrad Saunders in a booklet, Downton's Richest Family (1992).

7   *VCH Wiltshire* vol. XI.

8   It is not entirely clear whether any women voted before 1832. Before that date the law did not specify male voters, whereas after 1832 it did.

9   Report by George Manning 1831.

10   *VCH Wiltshire* vol. IV records the census population totals for the borough: 2,426 in 1801, 2,624 in 1811 and 3,114 in 1821.

11   Hunt T: *Building Jerusalem* (2004).

12   Southey R: *Book of the Church* (1824).

13   For the customs of Downton see Appendix 3.

14   Crowey D.A: 'The Manor Court of Downton in the 18th Century'. *WAM* 76 (1981).

[15] See Appendix 3.

[16] Enclosure entailed the reallocation of land previously held in open field strips and common land into consolidated fenced or hedged farms. It also led to a destruction of ancient customs and rights.

[17] WSA A1/210/80/EA85.

[18] *VCH Wiltshire* vol. IV.

[19] See Bettey, J H: *Wessex from AD 1000* for statistics on riots in Wessex as a whole.

[20] Chambers J: *Rebels in the Fields* (1995).

[22] Quoted in Newman R. 'The Swing Riots: Agricultural Revolt in 1830'. *Hatcher Review* vol. 2 no. 19.

[23] Chambers J. *Wiltshire Machine Breakers* (1993).

[24] www.historyofparliamentonline.org.

[25] Answers of the Returning Officer of the Borough of Downton to the Circular of 24th November 1831 from the Home Office.

[26] Antonia Fraser: Perilous Question, the drama of the Great Reform Bill 1832 (2013).

[27] *The Salisbury and Winchester Journal* June 11th, 1832.

[28] Eric Evans: *The Great Reform Act of 1832* (1983).

Chapter 7

[1] In 1841 the responsibility for recording population passed to the General Register Office and each census was completed on a single day. Previous population figures were based on reports by parish overseers and were usually compiled over several days.

[2] *VCH Wiltshire* vol. IV.

[3] The role of mayor of Downton originated from the mediaeval tithingman who was an appointee of the Lord of the Manor and who acted as the Lord's eyes and ears in the village. Later the term alderman came into use. The term mayor appears in the seventeenth century.

[4] Glynn E.F: 'Notes on Downton' *WSA* 3929/3.

[5] Woodford's unpublished history notes, *History of Downton,* were sold to raise funds for the Wessex Cancer Trust in the 1980s. Copies can be consulted in the Salisbury and Downton Libraries.

[6] The Downton mace used to be kept in the Memorial Hall and is now in Salisbury Museum.

[7] The Select Vestry was a committee which managed parochial affairs in large and populous parishes.

[8] www.thedowntonstory.com. Research by Ken Light, a Canadian citizen who is descended from Downton migrants.

[9] The emigration featured in the BBC television series by Michael Wood: *The Great British Story* (2012).

[10] See Appendix 5 for a complete list of migrants from Downton.

[11] www.elgin.ca

[12] From family history research by Margaret Smith.

Notes

[13] This letter is quoted in Waymouth, page 133. It also appears in Lucille H. Campey: 'Seeking a Better Future: The English Pioneers of Ontario and Quebec' (2012).

[14] Hurley B: *Rough Justice* (unpub) WSHC.

[15] Bettey's *Wessex from 1000AD* contains a good description of living conditions. The sanitary arrangements were still in evidence in the 1950s. Cottages of this description are remembered by many Downton inhabitants including the author

[16] Several accounts of Downton history mistakenly state that there was a cholera epidemic, including Waymouth's and Light's. These resulted from a misinterpretation of the Select Vestry Memorandum listing precautions should cholera appear.

[17] Memorandum of the Select Vestry 1832.

[18] At the time of writing this building houses a car repair shop.

[19] See also chapter 9.

[20] Green Lane is now a residential street again. For more on this see chapter 9.

[21] See chapter 10.

[22] For more information on working and social life see chapters 9 and 11.

[23] *VCH Wiltshire* vol. XI

[24] At the time of writing the building is a disused church hall.

[25] Between 1936 and 1964 it housed a senior school.

[26] See chapter 10.

[27] Lord Fellowes is the great grandson of Professor Wrightson. Several national newspapers reported in 2013 that a Downton publican received at least one customer a week visiting Downton to look for 'the Abbey'. The fictional series was in fact set in Yorkshire and filmed at Highclere Castle in Hampshire.

[28] The Museum of Surf, Braunton, Devon, has verified this story.

[29] Trafalgar House, originally Standlynch Park, was built in 1733 for Sir Peter Vanderput. In 1813 this estate was acquired by the nation and was given to the heir of Admiral Lord Nelson in recognition of the victory over the French in the Battle of Trafalgar.

[30] §See chapter 11

Chapter 8

[1] See chapter 9.

[2] David Lloyd George, Chancellor of the Exchequer in 1909.

[3] WSA uncatalogued, accession no. 4190/2013, donated by the author.

[4] British government recruitment posters contained images of Belgium as a helpless victim of German aggression in August 1914.

[5] Green E: *Downton and the First World War* (2002).

[6] The figures quoted by Waymouth are incorrect.

[7] Total servicemen in the First World War = 8.9 million, deaths = 908,000: Figures taken from www.historylearning.org.

[8] See chapter 12.

[9] The medals are now in the possession of the the author, whose mother,

Charles Weeks' nearest relative, discovered them.

[10] Edward James Blake was known as Jim to his friends. The underlining is his.

[11] Edward James Blake is buried in Achiet le Grand Communal Cemetery Extension, Grave no. II G 22.

[12] Green E: *Downton in the First World War*. Note that the motive for suicide is not recorded.

[13] The background stories of these three men have been included here because they do not appear in Edward Green's book.

[14] Harry Noble's papers were loaned by Ann Ireland.

[15] Information on Dr. B.L. Whitehead supplied by Dr. Miranda Whitehead.

[16] Most of the Tannery was demolished for a new development, Church Leat, in the 1970s except for the main building which was converted into flats.

[17] www.theroyalbritishlegion.org.uk.

[18] The letter does not contain an addressee. It was found among papers belonging to Joan Gwyther.

[19] There were twelve pence to a shilling and a shilling is five pence in modern money so his rabbits were bought for about three and a half pence and sold for about four pence, five pence or seven pence.

[20] Moot House was fully restored after the fire.

[21] See Appendix 5 for the full text of Gwen Burnham's memoir. describing the fire.

[22] See chapter 9.

[23] For a list of names see Appendix 4.

[24] Additional information provided by the Historical Society of Ottawa. The author has been unable to find more details of this incident.

[25] The incident was reported in the *Salisbury and Winchester Journal*, April 17th 1942 although in 2012 when a plaque was unveiled modern press reports wrote of a cover-up. See for example the *Bath Chronicle*, April 11, 2012.

[27] Dennis Musselwhite and Margaret Smith.

[28] *Downton WI Scrapbook* (1956).

[29] The story of her father was provided by Pat Cameron.

[30] Details of the Whitehead family were provided by Dr. Miranda Whitehead.

[31] Interview with Dennis Musselwhite.

[32] See chapter 1.

[33] The figures are difficult to verify as boundary changes mean that in 1951 Redlynch was included though they seem to be approximately correct. See *VCH Wiltshire* vol. IV.

[34] *Salisbury Journal*, 10th Jan 1958.

[35] Wick House School was run by Mrs. Grenfell, in Wick House. It was the former home of the Bonvalots and housed a private girls' preparatory school from 1949 until 1964.

[36] See chapter 9.

[37] Whitmarsh J. and Ireland A: *Memories of Dad and Downton Station* (2011).

[38] See chapter 10.

[39] See chapter 11.

[40] See chapter 12.

Notes

41 *Salisbury Journal*, August 1 2002.

Chapter 9

1   Interview with Bert Blake.
2   www.history.wiltshire.gov.uk and VCH Wiltshire vol. XI. The South Wiltshire
    Industrial Archaeology Society, who carried out a survey of Downton Tannery
    shortly before its conversion to residential use, claim on their website that
    there is evidence of tanning in 1215 but when contacted by the author they
    could not verify the source.
3   *VCH Wiltshire* vol. XI.
4   Sometimes known as Wild Weir, it was constructed to raise the level of the
    river to allow water to run off into the mill stream.
5   *VCH Wiltshire* vol. XI.
6   Interview with Les Ridgeley.
7   *VCH Wiltshire* vol. XI.
8   Page M. *The Pipe Roll of the Bishop of Winchester 1301-2* (1996). Titow in
    his translation of the 1324-5 roll in English Rural Society found the same
    situation just over twenty years later. This seems odd, given that fulling mills
    were highly profitable. As they rapidly caught on during this area at the time,
    perhaps there were just too many landlords offering more attractive terms.
9   *VCH Wiltshire* vol. XI and vol. IV.
10 Now known as Waterside Mill.
11 *Southern Beam* no. 10, Volume 7 (1956). The magazine was produced for the
    employees of the Southern Division of the Central Electricity Authority.
12 Now Mill House, 144 The Borough.
13 'The Downton Lace Industry', Gibson M. *Hatcher Review* vol. 8.
14 Salisbury Museum and also Hartley S. & Parry P: Downton Lace: *A History
    of Lacemaking in Salisbury and the Surrounding Area* (1991). For Downton lace
    patterns see Kemp B. *Downton Lace* (1988).
15 *Downton WI Scrapbook* (1956).
16 *VCH Wiltshire* vol. XI.
17 *Universal British Directory* (1793).
18 The three cottages now form a single property known as Creel Cottage.
19 Eastman Family History website.
20 In 1723 this Act of Parliament stated that a person claiming poor relief had to
    enter a workhouse and do a set amount of work.
21 *VCH Wiltshire* vol. XI.
22 *VCH Wiltshire* vol. XI.

Chapter 10

1   Peniston wrote over 7000 letters, many of which have been published by the
    Wiltshire Record Society. During the Swing Riots in November 1830 he
    wrote extensively of preparing his troop to deal with the disturbances and
    riots in the area, although he does not mention Downton specifically. Cowan
    M. (ed): *The Letters of John Peniston, Architect, Catholic and Yeomanry Officer,*

1823-1830. WRS vol.50 (1996)

2   *WI Scrapbook* (1956).

3   The sketch is in the British Museum collection and cannot be reproduced here.

4   See chapter 2.

5   www.downtonbuildings.

6   Bray, N: *The Salisbury and Dorset Junction Railway* (2010) Kestrel

7   Whitmarsh J and Ireland *A: Memories of Dad and Downton Station.* See the frontispiece for a photograph of Harry Hepper selling the last train ticket at Downton station.

Chapter 11

1   See chapter 2.

2   *VCH Wiltshire* vol. XI.

3   See chapter 4.

4   For a full description of the church and listed features in the churchyard see *VCH Wiltshire* Vol XI, www.southwilts.com/downtonbuildings.

5   Bettey J.H: *Wessex from AD1000* (1986).

6   See chapter 5.

7   The term given to Protestants who dissented from the established Church of England.

8   Bettey: *Rural Life in Wessex 1500-1900* (1988).

9   J. Chandler: (ed) 'Wiltshire Dissenters' Meeting House Certificates and Registrations 1689-1852', *WRS* vol. 40 (1985) and email from Dr. Rosalind Johnson, Winchester University.

10 Chandler J. *Endless Street* (1983).

11 *VCH Wiltshire* vol. XI and Titow J.Z: *English Rural Society* (1969).

12 www.history.ac.uk/cmh/gaz/gazweb2/html: Gazetter of Markets and Fairs to 1516.

13 As note 12.

14 Although J. H. Bettey states they were held in April and September, Local Historian vol. 34, no. 4.

15 Green E: *Downton and the First World War* (2002)

16 Green E: *Downton and the First World War* (2002)

17 Green E: *Downton and the First World War* (2002)

18 Interview with Don Moody.

19 *High Jinks: Moot* Preservation Trust (undated).

20 The first modern Cuckoo Fair was the subject of a short documentary made by Southern Television in the series, Country Ways.

21 www.history.wiltshire.gov.uk/community cites a Downton legend that villagers were surprised that the cuckoo escaped from the pound, which was simply a fenced enclosure, although the author has never previously encountered this story and it may have been told as a piece of self-deprecating local humour.

Notes

Chapter 12

[1]   Cowan M: *Wiltshire Water Meadows* (2005).

[2]   Taylor J: *A Discovery by Wherry from London to Salisbury* (1623) cited in J. Chandler:' John Taylor makes a voyage to Salisbury in 1623', *Hatcher Review* vol. 4 no. 40 (1995).

[3]   Cross D: 'Salisbury as a Seaport'. *Sarum Chronicle* 3 (2003).

[4]   Bettey J.H: *Wiltshire Farming in the 17th Century* WRS vol. 57 (2005).

[5]   Defoe D: *A Tour through the Whole Island of Great Britain* (1724-7).

[6]   WSA 490/842.

[7]   WSA 490/909.

[8]   WSA 490/890.

[9]   Bettey J.H: 'Sheep and Corn, Seventeenth Century Farming in the Salisbury District', *Sarum Chronicle* 2, (2002).

[10] Steele N: 'Sir Joseph Ashe, Bt. 1617-1686, an Advocate of Watermeadows in Good Husbandry', *Hatcher Review* vol. 2 no. 13 (1982).

[11] Green E: *Downton and the First World War* (2002). It should be stated that the seriousness of a particular flood depends very much on personal experience which accounts for some discrepancies between reports and memory.

[12] www.bbc.co.uk/wiltshire/villages/downton

Sources

This book is not intended as an academic work of reference or scholarship and therefore it is hoped that the reader does not need to be informed of the source of every assertion. Neither would this be feasible given that much of the data relating to local and national history is the result of a lifetime of study. However it would be frustrating for the general reader if there was no indication of works and documents consulted. Printed below is a list of major sources.

British and International History

Ceasar J. *De Bello Gallico* (2013 ed.)
Evans A. *The Great Reform Act of 1832* (1994)
Frazer A. *Perilous Question; The Drama of the Great Reform Bill 1832* (2013)
Howlett R. *Chronicles of the Reigns of Stephen, Henry II and Richard I* (1989 ed.)
Horne P. *The Rural World 1780-1850* (1980)
Hunt T. *Building Jerusalem* (2005)
Oxford Dictionary of National Biography (2004)
Marr A. *History of the World* (2013)
Schama S. *History of Britain* (2002)
Tacitus. *Agricola* Book I (2010ed.)
Titow J. Z. *English Rural Society 1200-1350* (1969)
Vinogradoff P. *Oxford Studies in Social and Legal History* vol. 5. (1916)
Warren W.L. *Henry II* (2000)
Wood M. *In Search of England* (2000)
Wood M. *The Great British Story* BBC DVD (2012)

Local History Books and Records

Bettey J.H. *Wessex from AD 1000* (1986)
Bettey J.H. *Rural Life in Wessex 1500-1900* (1987)
Bray N. *The Salisbury and Dorset Junction Railway* (2010)
Chambers J. *The Wiltshire Machine Breakers* (1993)

Sources

Chambers J. *Rebels of the Fields* (1995)

Chandler J. *Endless Street, A History of Salisbury and its People* (1983)

Chandler J. (ed.) *Wiltshire Dissenters Meeting House Certificates and Registrations 1689-1852.* WRS No.40 (1985)

Cowan M. *Wiltshire Water Meadows* (2005)

Cunliffe B. *Danebury; Anatomy of a Hill Fort* (1983)

Cunnington B.H. *Records of the County of Wilts, being extracts from the Quarter Sessions Great Rolls of the 17th Century* (1932)

Finberg H.P.R. *Early Charters of Wessex* (1964)

Hare J. *A Prospering Society; Wiltshire in the Later Middle Ages.* (2011)

Hurley B. *Rough Justice* (1999)

Page M. (ed) The Pipe Roll of the Bishopric of Winchester 1301-2 (1996)

Page M. (ed) The Pipe Roll of the Bishopric of Winchester 1409-10 (1999)

Slocombe I. *Wiltshire Quarter Sessions Order Book 1642-54* WRS no. 67 (2014)

Victoria County History: *Wiltshire*, vols. IV,V and XI

Wright G.N. *Roads and Trackways of Wessex* (1988)

The Very Best of Time Team Digs. Channel 4 DVD (2006)

Downton

Downton Moot Preservation Trust: *High Jinks in the Moot* (undated)

Downton Heritage Trail Booklet (2009)

Downton Women's Institute Scrapbook WSA. (1956)

Glynn E.F. *Notes on Downton* (WSA 3929/3)

Green E. *Downton and the First World War* (2002)

Hartley S. & Parry P. *Downton Lace: A History of Lacemaking in Salisbury and the Surrounding Area* (1991)

Middleton A. & Blake B. *Reflections (We Remember the Downton where we were Born)* (undated)

Saunders C. et al. *Downton's Richest Family* (1992)

Squarey E.P. *The Moot and its Traditions* (undated [1906])

Whitmarsh J. and Ireland A. *Memories of Dad and Downton Station* (2011)

Waymouth D. *Downton, 7000 Years of an English Village* (1999)

Woodford R. *History of Downton* (undated)

Articles

Beresford M.W. The Six New Towns of the Bishop of Winchester,1200-1255. *Medieval Archaeology* vol. 3 (1959)

Bettey J. Sheep and Corn, 17th Century Farming in the Salisbury District. *Sarum Chronicle* No.2 (2002)

Chandler J. John Taylor Makes a Voyage from London to Salisbury in 1623. *Hatcher Review* Vol 4. no. 40. (1995)

Cross D. Salisbury as a Seaport. *Sarum Chronicle* no.3 (2003)

Du Boulay Hill Rev. A. The Saxon Boundaries of Downton. *WAM* no. 36 (1909-10)

Floyer J.K. Passages from the History of Downton. *WAM* No.29 (1896-97)

Gibson M. The Downton Lace Industry. *Hatcher Review* Vol.8

Giles J.A. (ed.) William of Malmesbury: History of the Norman Kings (1847)

Hinton D. Tannery House Archaeological Report. Wessex Archaeology Report. no. 463

Howlett R: Chronicles of the Reigns of Stephen, Henry II and Richard I (1884)

Newman R. The Swing Riots: Agricultural Revolution 1830. *Hatcher Review* Vol.2 No.19

Oxford Dictionary of National Biography (2004)

Rahtz P.A. Neolithic and Beaker Sites at Downton, Salisbury. *Wiltshire Archaeological Newsletter* (1960)

Rahtz P.A. A Roman Villa at Downton. *WAM* No.58 (1960)

Rahtz P.A. Saxon and Medieval Features at Downton. *WAM* no. 59 (1961)

Riall N. Hampshire in Anarchy, 1142-1153; The Role of Bishop Henry de Blois. *Hatcher Review* vol. 4 No.37

Steele N. Sir Joseph Ashe, Bt. 1617-1686, An Advocate of Watermeadows in Good Husbandry. *Hatcher Review* Vol 2 no. 3 (1982)

Websites

Many primary and secondary sources can be accessed via the websites listed below.

www.ancestry.co.uk (Censuses, birth marriage and death records, emigration records and more)

www.historyofparliamentonline.org.uk (Biographies of MPs / parliamentary history)

www.british-history.ac.uk (Victoria County History and other resources)

www.wiltshirerecordsociety.org.uk (Published Wiltshire resources on line)

www.archive.com (Digital library which includes the WAM)

www.heritagegateway.org.uk (Listed buildings)

www.placenames.org.uk (Origin of place-names)

www.downtonbuildings.org.uk (Listing of all Downton buildings)

Sources

www.southwilts.com (Community website)
bw.   history.wiltshire.gov.uk (Brief histories of communities)
www.domesdaymap.co.uk/Downton (Domesday Book)
www.englishheritage.org.uk (Monuments and listed buildings)
www.thedowntonstory.com (Canadian emigration)
www.angelfire.com (Eastman family website)
www.batlefieldstrust.com (military history)

Miscellaneous
Eaves M.E.D. Agricultural Water Management in the English Landscape:
    a Case Study of Downton, Wiltshire. (2009)
Environment Agency. Defending Downton
Wilton House: The Home of the Earl of Pembroke

Index

Illustrations are denoted in bold type

Index

Index

Index

Index

Lightning Source UK Ltd.
Milton Keynes UK
UKOW07n1957011115

261862UK00004B/49/P